IMAGES

HISTORIC AMHERST

PAULINE M. FURLONG

NIMBUS
PUBLISHING

Nimbus Publishing Limited
PO Box 9166
Halifax, NS B3K 5M8
(902) 455-4286

Printed and bound in Canada

Designer: Joan Sinclair

Front cover: Taken in the early 1900s, this photograph shows the corner of Victoria and Church streets, which continues to serve as the hub of the downtown core in the town of Amherst.

Title page: Amherst's Victoria Street has served pedestrians, horse-drawn buggies, and new-fangled motorized vehicles over centuries of use as the town's main thoroughfare. This streetscape shows the Two Barkers' department store (now Margolian's) and a bevy of shops that made up the commercial district in the 1900s.

National Library of Canada Cataloguing in Publication Data

Furlong, Pauline, M. (Pauline Marie), 1966-
Historic Amherst
(Images of our past)
ISBN 1-55109-383-9

1. Amherst (N.S.)—History—Pictorial works. I. Title.
II. Series.

FC2499.A43F87 2001 971.6'11 C2001-903194-7
F1039.5.A14F87 2001

Canada

The Canada Council for the Arts | Le Conseil des Arts du Canada

We acknowledge the financial support of the Government of Canada through the Book Publishing Industry Development Program (BPIDP) and the Canada Council for our publishing activities.

For my mother

Acknowledgements

Just as it takes a village to raise a child, it may be said that it takes a community to launch a book. This project is not unique in that respect and my appreciation goes out to a number of people who so graciously donated time, energy, and expertise in helping to research and document the early pictorial history of Amherst. In particular, I extend my thanks to Cumberland County Museum curator Barb Thompson, Terri Kinnear, Glenna Everill, and all the volunteers who were able to provide insight into the town during the period from the late 1800s to 1945; to Gary Shutlak at the Public Archives of Nova Scotia; to Ron Elliott, Deane Allen, Lucie Martin-Bishop, Donna Morse, and Janet S. Christie, all of whom contributed photographs, memories, and histories; and to Carl LeBlanc and Diane Kinnear, whose careful attention to detail is evident in each image included. In particular, I also thank John McKay, whose keen editing eye, wealth of knowledge about local history, and interest in minute details were invaluable. Last but certainly not least, I express a great debt of gratitude to my husband, Donald, and our daughter, Mia Elizabeth. Their unwavering support during the research, writing, and editing period was indispensable.

Pauline Furlong

Contents

Introduction

We showed him all the city's pride
Our streets, and towers, and harbors wide
Yet not for these his woodsman's eyes
Gleamed once with wonder or surprise;
He looked our latest marvels through
And heard more tongues than Babel knew
Unmoved; his homesick thoughts afar
Still roamed the shores of Tantramar

William Hervey Woods

If history is indeed the sum of its parts, it may well be that the community lying at the southern fringe of the great salt marshes of Tantramar comprises a microcosm befitting the adage. The district surrounding the town of Amherst in northern Nova Scotia speaks eloquently of a past fraught with struggle and hope, with the upheaval of conquest and the disruption of a long-established way of life. It has the dubious distinction of being witness to the opening moves in 150 years of imperialistic struggle for domination of a continent.

Amherst, the shiretown of Cumberland County, lies sprawled across two parallel ridges running east-west above the southern edge of the Amherst marsh, a division of the Tantramar marshes, an 85-square-mile area of salt marsh fanning out from the shores of Cumberland Basin at the northern head of the Bay of Fundy. The area of the marshes comprises the western third of the 17-mile Isthmus of Chignecto, the neck of land that attaches peninsular Nova Scotia to the mainland.

Following its earliest non-native settlement, the isthmus became a strategic area during the eighteenth-century struggle for European domination of North America. Prior to the arrival of Europeans into the region, it was a vast empty solitude of wind-waved salt marsh grasses and silent virgin forests. Laced by slow, meandering streams, expanses of bog land and caribou plain, and miles of ancient moose pasture amid serene forested uplands that had flourished virtually untouched in the wake of the retreating ice of the last glaciation, it was a natural paradise. The Mi'kmaq would visit on a seasonal basis, arriving to fish the pelagic Gaspereaux, to trap furs in the marshes, and to partake of the unimaginable swarms of wildfowl that frequented the brackish lowlands during their spring and fall migrations.

Native oral history indicates that, for centuries, the Mi'kmaq encamped each year on the southern ridge above the marsh, establishing a principal village site which they called *Nemalooscudaagan*, near the meandering tidal creek in the marsh where it flowed past the foot of the slope. Another village site, farther to the west, was named *Weehakage*, and the stream in the marsh was called *Mascoudgain*. The latter—now named Laplanche River and altered significantly from its original course—also provided the natives with a water route. This was broken only by a few short portages, from Cumberland Basin to the Tidnish River, the latter flowing eastward to salt water on the far side of the isthmus.

Early in the seventeenth century, the French, who became known as Acadians, established settlements along the shores of the Bay of Fundy. Many of these first settlers originated in the Loudun district of western France, springing from the ranks of Catholic farmers who worked the low-lying land along the river Loire and its tributaries, land that required constant vigilance against incursion by the flooding river. The Acadians' unique system of dykes and aboiteaux for controlling tidal inundation of the salt marshes adjacent to the tidal rivers of the Bay of Fundy was a direct result of the experience they gained in France.

Early reconnaissance of the upper bay determined that the Chignecto region was a huge pasture capable of supporting herds of horned cattle. Nonetheless, it wasn't until 1672 that the Bourgeois family and five others departed the overcrowded settlements at Port Royal and landed below the ridge lying at the confluence of a pair of rivers rising to the east in the great marshes.

The village of Beaubassin, established near the western end of the Fort Lawrence Ridge, was the first European settlement in the Chignecto region. Over the next eighty-three years, a number of satellite enclaves sprang up between the northern slopes of the Amherst ridge, eastward along the Fort Lawrence ridge, and as far west as the Aulac ridge, Sackville, and Shepody, as well as at Baie Verte and the Northumberland shore. By the time of Le Grand Dérangement—The Expulsion—in 1755, the population had increased to the point that one thousand Acadian inhabitants were transported down Cumberland Basin from Chignecto. British military efficiency notwithstanding, many others escaped.

From its humble beginning in the seventeenth century, Old Acadia fell to the British no less than four times, but peace negotiations always returned it to France. However, after its final loss to the British in 1710, the 1713 Treaty of Utrecht did not restore Old Acadia to French control. The treaty failed to adequately define the western boundary between what the British claimed as Nova Scotia, and the wilderness territory to the west, leading to the fatal reduction of Old Acadia. Nonetheless, the treaty did permit France to retain possession of the principal islands in the Gulf of St. Lawrence, including Isle-St. Jean (Prince Edward Island) and Isle Royale (Cape Breton).

During the years following the treaty, the Acadians living on the isthmus prospered, despite British New England's claim to the lucrative North Atlantic fishery, and their control of the Gulf of St. Lawrence. However, by the early 1720s, British control was aggressively opposed by the burgeoning French fortress town of Louisbourg, on Isle Royale. Whoever controlled the gulf held the key to control of the interior, and with Louisbourg assuming guardianship of the gulf of St. Lawrence, the British were distracted from their concerns with the collection of benign peasant farmers at Chignecto.

France also neglected the now-isolated Acadia due to its preoccupation with the gulf fishery and the settlements of New France along the St. Lawrence and westward. As hostilities grew over the next quarter century, Louisbourg fell to the British in 1845 through the instigation of New England. Raiding excursions were carried out into the Bay of Fundy all the way to Chignecto. Meanwhile, the Acadians continued to trade with whomever they could, New Englanders included, maintaining the overland route through the isthmus at Chignecto and even continuing their supply of goods to the captured Louisbourg. Unbelievably, the Treaty of Aix-La-Chapelle in 1748 returned Louisbourg to the French.

The following year, the British established a settlement at Chebucto (Halifax), and in 1750, on his second attempt, Charles Lawrence constructed a fort on the British side of the Missaquash River near the Acadian village of Beaubassin, with a view to controlling the local Acadians, now subjects of the British King. The previous attempt had failed because of French and Mi'kmaq resistance, but not before the buildings in Beaubassin were in flames, and the cattle driven across the west bank of the river. In 1751, perhaps emboldened by the return of Louisbourg, France asserted its sovereignty by claiming the Missaquash River as the eastern border of New France and building a fort on a promontory on the west side, some three thousand yards across the marsh from Fort Lawrence. The French also constructed Fort Gaspereaux at Baie Verte, on the gulf side of the isthmus, ostensibly to guard the overland route to Louisbourg and to assert their command of the territory west of the arbitrary border of Old Acadia which, they concluded, belonged to New France since it was not part of Nova Scotia.

Over the next four years, with an ever-increasing British presence in Nova Scotia, the French military posturing in Chignecto was ineffective, while the dispossessed Acadians longed for any kind of compromise that would see them return to their lands across the Missaquash. The people freely contemplated a pledge of neutrality rather than outright allegiance to the British crown, provided they could refrain from taking up arms against their own countrymen in the event of future conflict. This, of course, was unacceptable to the British who would have to regard them as loyal subjects or enemy aliens in the event of war. It was a futile wish on the part of the Acadians since they faced the threat of the enigmatic priest, Abbé Jean Louis Le Loutre, to loose the Mi'kmaq upon any of them choosing to cooperate with the despised British.

In the summer of 1755, the British set in motion their plan to reduce the continental outposts of New France in the east, south, and west. Thus, the move that would prove fatal to Old Acadia was made against Fort Beausejour. After 150 years of uncertain tenure, of being tossed between British pillar and French post, the axe fell on the Acadians, the least aggressive of people, who were now swept up in the conflict that would signal the beginning of the British conquest of the entire continent.

In late fall of that year, when the British transports sailed down Cumberland Basin carrying one thousand expelled Chignecto Acadians toward an uncertain future, Abbé Le Loutre, who had proclaimed that it would be better to be buried under the ruins of the fort than surrender, was nowhere to be found. He had abandoned his Mi'kmaq followers, as he had deserted his devout, God-fearing Acadians.

Following the expulsion and the eventual reduction of Louisbourg in 1758, the remainder of British military operations in the east could be characterized as a final mopping up. By then, it was recognized that the cleared, arable, and cultivated Acadian lands—in excess of 100,000 acres, some of which had been under cultivation for 150 years—should be promoted as incentive to resettling the under-populated Nova Scotia, particularly in the south and west, including Chignecto.

The Acadian settlements east of the Missaquash languished in abandonment. The British, abandoning as well the inferior, hastily constructed Fort Lawrence, occupied Fort Beausejour immediately following its surrender and renamed it Fort Cumberland. The razed village of Beaubassin, whose ruins lay on the drumlin land below Fort Lawrence, was never reoccupied during the subsequent resettlement. Its location was eventually lost, particularly to new settlers in the district who had never known of its existence, until more than a century later when excavation of the railway cutting through the foot of Fort Lawrence Ridge unearthed a number of graves in the long-lost village burying ground.

To the southeast across the marsh, the old Indian-Acadian trail coming up from Minas Basin and passing along the ridge and on toward the Gulf shore to the east was devoid of traffic, and the old fields lay fallow and abandoned. On the lower marshes, those dyked enclaves closest to Cumberland Basin and the estuaries of the Laplanche and Missaquash rivers, the haylands lay uncut and the hay staddles empty.

By September 1759, when the decisive battle had been won on the Plains of Abraham, grants had been issued for the establishment of townships along the eastern shore of the Bay of Fundy and across the Isthmus of Chignecto. This resulted in the survey of the 34,500-acre (approximately 54-square mile) Cumberland Grant in 1763, lying between the Aulac and Laplanche rivers, and the laying out of the Amherst township on the south side of the Laplanche, about two miles west of the current town site.

The original township was surveyed by British military engineers and named by Joseph Morse for Lord Jeffrey Amherst. A little-known supply colonel, Amherst had never been to North America before he was promoted to major general and arrived at Halifax in 1758 to lead the final siege of Louisbourg. The township received Amherst's name, in keeping with the British tradition of naming places after their heroes, although it is doubtful that Amherst ever saw the Chignecto region.

The location selected for the township favoured the lower, more easily cultivated area lying between the high ridges to the east, the marshes to the north—some of which had been dyked by the Acadians—

Old magazine, Fort Cumberland

THE OFFICERS' QUARTERS AT FORT CUMBERLAND

and Amherst Point and the Maccan River, to the west and south.

Amherst township had the edge over the original Acadian settlement at Beaubassin across the marsh because of the long-established trail coming up from Minas Basin. The trail permitted access to the untouched woodlands south of the marshes, which offered excellent mast and spar timber for British Admiralty surveyors. In the apportioning of land, the township offered each settler an amount of woodland, fertile and easily cultivated farmland, and dyked or partially dyked marshland for hay production and pasturing. In contrast, the site of Beaubassin—but a few hundred yards east of the riverine estuaries at Cumberland Basin—was a desolate and relatively non-productive expanse of turbid tidal channels and forlorn, wind-blown headlands, offering no room for expansion except eastward along Fort Lawrence Ridge.

While an office for the registry of land titles was opened at Fort Cumberland in February 1764, the first transfer of lands in the town of Amherst did not occur until August 22, 1768 when Ebenezer Fitch, then the captain of the militia, exchanged lots with Simon Fitch. A census taken in the village the previous year showed the population of Amherst being made up of sixty-eight males and fifty-seven females; most were of Irish descent, with only four being Acadian. As the Yorkshire immigrants continued to settle in Amherst, a church was built, along with two shops, a large tavern, a whipping post, and a blacksmith shop.

Eventually, a coach road was opened between Truro and Amherst, passing by the Wentworth Valley, River Philip, and Brookdale via the old Halifax Road (now Willow Street) before arriving on the Amherst ridge at Morse's Corner. Practical-minded villagers gradually led the movement to shift the village—laid out in neat rows on the road to Joggins near Christ Church Cemetery—near to Amherst Corners. This was accomplished over three years with almost every building being clustered around a new site where the present town is located. Three stores took up residence at the Corners, and soon, there were two blacksmith shops.

The newly-relocated settlement was supposed to be called Amherst, but not everyone called it that for quite some time. Almost universally, local residents of small rural areas tend to create their own names for places, and those early inhabitants of Amherst proved no different. Many people ignored the chosen name and simply referred to it as Morse's Corner, after Alpheus Morse. His father, Joseph Morse of Dedham, Massachusetts had been a commissary supply officer who served under Amherst in the Seven Years' War. And while the senior Morse never lived in Amherst, his son erected a house at the corner of Victoria and Willow streets. Two other early settlers—John Bent and Elisha Freeman—also settled with Alpheus on lands stretching from Morse's Corner to Etters Brook.

Most of the earliest homes constructed in this area were simple structures. One of the first was the Judge Morse homestead, which was built in 1775 and remained standing until the summer of 1908 when it was torn down. A bit of history went with it since it was in this structure than the Duke of Kent, father of the late Queen Victoria, and other men of high rank stayed during their visits to the Amherst area.

Throughout this time, Morse's Corner remained busy. The Nova Scotia Legislature in 1829 stated that a two-horse coach was all that was needed between Amherst and Truro and that it need run but once a week. By 1838, there were three thousand people in the Amherst area, some of whom signed a petition in 1841 for a coach service from Truro to Amherst after noting that an Amherst to Saint John coach had been operating since 1836. They wrote: "It is not creditable to this province that space should be the only one on the main roads of it and New Brunswick on which a comfortable and convenient passage cannot be had." Their efforts did not fall on deaf ears: by 1842, a Mr. Caldwell was operating two two-horse coaches between Truro and Amherst semi-weekly.

From 1847 onward, Charles Archibald of Truro and his partner, a Mr. Stevenson, held the contract for the coach service and by 1852 they were making the run three times a week. The road was improved each year, and by 1860 a coach left Truro every morning except Sunday, immediately following the arrival of the train from Halifax. Dr. D.A. Steele writes: "In late November, 1867, Archibald and Purdy's stagecoach picked us up at Truro at 11:00 A.M. Three passengers were on board bound to Amherst. There had been a few day's sleighing but now it was the 'reign of mud.' We plodded along through snow, Folly and Great Village and by nightfall had made Purdy's Inn at Westchester. Then slowly, steadily, we descended and reached Amherst via Morse's Corner at 2:00 A.M. having made the trip in 15 hours. We proceeded to the Cumberland Hotel and here we had an excellent supper. The price of passage was $5.00 with meals en route costing 75 cents."

The arrival of the first train in Amherst on November 11, 1872 effectively ended the coaching days that had proved so integral to the early building of the town. The generation which had refused to call the town by its given name had passed on, and the Morse's Corner and Amherst Corners names were dropped in favour of simply Amherst, a village well on its way to becoming a small town and service centre for the agricultural region.

A cursory look at Amherst in 1889, approximately halfway through its rise to economic prosperity, would reveal the following: a railway station serving five trains a day; the largest building construction and woodworking firm in eastern Canada, Rhodes, Curry; Robb's Foundry & Machine Works; Christie's Baggage Factory on Christie's Pond; Dominion Casket Factory; Amherst Boot & Shoe Factory; Amherst Motor Works (McKay car); Amherst Brick Yard; Donald's Redstone Quarry, on Willow Street; Church Street Quarry; McGrath & King Monument Works; Tingley's Granite Works; two weekly newspapers, *The Amherst Gazette* and the *Maritime Sentinel*; Lusby's Grist Mill, on Dickie Brook; a tannery, farther upstream; Electric Light Plant; McLean Milling Company; Delahunt & Savage Carriage Factory; Blacking Company; Hewson Woolen Mill; Victor Wood Works; seven foundries; Amherst Piano Factory; Amherst Mineral Water Company; Amherst Music Hall; a Y.M.C.A.; a community water supply system; Amherst Academy; Bank of Nova Scotia; a post office and customs house; the county courthouse and jail; the lay library; The Medical Hall and other pharmacies; numerous medical doctors, lawyers, and attorneys; several hotels and hostelries; a number of restaurants, oyster bars, and saloons; Carl Pridham's photography business; Max Stern's musical instruments, lessons offered; millinery, tailor, and dry goods shops; butcher shops, grocery, fish, and specialty shops; a hardware store, jewellery store, several blacksmith and farrier shops; numerous small shops; business services; and several churches.

Amherst had been thriving a good while prior to 1888 when the dream of Henry George Clopper Ketchum to build the Chignecto Ship Railway to carry ships across the isthmus began to take shape. The final plan called for a dead straight line. There had been an earlier plan that proposed to run closer to Amherst while utilizing the first mile or so of the Laplanche River. This plan died because it required unavoidable changes of direction that were almost impossible to incorporate. The final right of way was 17 miles, 240 feet from the shore of Cumberland Basin to Baie Verte (which opens on Northumberland Strait). Ships of no more than two thousand deadweight tons—roughly one thousand tons for the ship and the same for the cargo—were the limit of the railway, with the sectional design of the transporters permitting ships of smaller size to be transported. Ships were also limited by their dimensions: no more than 235 feet long, 56 feet wide, and drawing 15 feet of water.

The labour force, from mid-1889 to the end of 1890, ranged upward to some four thousand men, primarily on the roadbed. Amherst at the time had about 3,500 inhabitants and a fully-employed workforce. Most of the ship railway labour was imported, drawing upon seasonal railway workers in the region and from Quebec. There was also a large Italian contingent of itinerant railway workers. Amherst could neither accommodate nor feed them, and various camps were set up along the line at strategic locations. The Italians established one of these, Smoky Hollow Camp, beside the railway in the vicinity of the Chappelle Farmstead, in Tidnish. Construction of the railway proceeded for thirty-four months until the summer of 1891, when funds dried up and the work gradually came to a halt.

However, by 1910 when Amherst celebrated Old Home Week, the population had risen to five thousand, and the town was as prosperous and optimistic about the future as it ever would be again. While business and industry continued to grow, subtle forces were also at work eroding the strength of the boom during the years before the Great War, an erosion that would not be felt in any alarming way until that horrendous conflict was over. In the meantime, Robb's constructed a structural steel fabrication plant in 1904, and a piano factory was soon to be constructed on the Sackville Road. The Amherst Foundry complex was also constructed on Station Street, and the Malleable Iron Foundry was operating beside the railway on upper Park Street. Then, too, the McKay automobile was being manufactured in the Amherst Motor Works just prior to the beginning of the Great War.

The 1910 Old Home Week celebration was a gala time for the town and for the hundreds of former citizens who returned for the celebrations. People were urged to invite friends and relations from away to come

Aerial photo of Amherst, c.1946

home for the great week, and many did. A record of the times states that on the closing night of the celebrations, some fifteen thousand people (three times Amherst's population) witnessed the fireworks display over Christie's Pond. The pond, with its floating bandstand, provided a fabulous reflecting pool for the spectacle.

Following the Great War, things began to wind down. While the war had meant temporary prosperity for some firms, and steady employment for others, the quickly expanding industrial base of central Canada, with its high population density and close proximity to large markets, was beginning to take its toll on Maritime industry. Aside from fishing, lumbering, and coal mining, there was little of eastern industry that couldn't be duplicated and even expanded more cheaply in central Canada and Quebec. As well, the capitalistic system of business financing (wherein companies were controlled by boards of directors selected for their efficiency in cutting costs and reaping a maximum return to investors) was also taking its toll.

Under the old system, modernization was slow or non-existent. A plant was allowed to wear out or become obsolete because the slow, inefficient methods of production could not keep up with demands. To eliminate the competition, larger firms from away began buying up businesses and either closing them or reducing them to skeleton operations or minor branch plants. Family-owned businesses were reluctant to expand or modernize, since it meant spending money from the private family fortune rather than from the financial equity of a corporately-constructed industry. Since there were few effective labour unions and no severance or pension considerations for the workers, firms could be sold or closed on short notice. A subtle erosion of Amherst's industrial base, coupled with the distance and freight rates to viable markets and raw materials, gradually helped bring the town and the entire eastern region to their present level.

Historic Amherst is intended to document the transition from a parochial community through the boom and bust economic times into the twentieth century. Beginning with the late 1880s, this pictorial account chronicles the expansion and decline of the border town through years of "Busy Amherst" and the gradual decline of its industrial base. If a picture is worth a thousand words, then this collection should serve as a testimonial to younger generations about Amherst's early prosperity, as well as its social, sporting, recreational, and agrarian past. In the words of Robery A. Heinlein, "A generation that ignores history has no past and no future."

Chapter 1

Downtown Amherst

VICTORIA STREET

Originally known as Main Street, this well-travelled route was renamed in honour of warm-hearted Queen Victoria shortly after her succession to the throne in 1837 at age 18. The town's original site was laid out on the road to Joggins near Christ Church Cemetery, but practical-minded area residents opted to move closer to the more convenient Amherst Corners, making Victoria Street part of the downtown trading centre. Nearly everything consumers needed was clustered in or near this main street. The middle left of this photograph shows the landmark spire of the First Baptist Church. Across the street are Moss Jewellers, the original Bank of Nova Scotia, the Rhodes-Steele Block, and R.C. Fuller and Company's drugstore on the corner of Church Street.

Victoria Street in the late 1800s

The photograph description, *Amherst, NS (40 years ago)*, refers to 40 years prior to 1926, which means there were no Jubilee trees (planted in 1887, some of which are still there) in Courthouse Square; the old burned courthouse (lower left) had yet to be replaced (1888) and the Black, Moffatt, and Hickman blocks, along with the new Tupper pharmacy, all on the right of the photograph, had not yet been built. Drivers parked their rigs where they pleased along this route. In fact, it would be another 30 years before the law forced traffic to the righthand side of the street. As well, the wires seen on poles here were telegraph wires since the electric light plant wasn't built until 1888, and the only telephones in town were in the two connecting Robb's retail stores on Victoria Street with the plant on Lower Laplanche Street.

EARLY VICTORIA STREET

At first, temperance usually involved a promise not to drink spirits, leaving members of so-called temperance houses at liberty to consume wine and beer at their discretion. However, by the mid-1850s, temperance societies began advocating the much stronger position of teetotalism in temperance houses such as this one on Victoria Street. Meanwhile, the town's first Methodist Church is on the left side of the street in this photograph. It was later moved to Station Street to make way for a new stone church. The low fence in the right foreground surrounds the lawn of the Terrace Hotel, which dominated the corner of Victoria and Station streets.

Bird's eye view

This view from St. Stephen's Church tower, taken in mid-afternoon judging from the shadows, shows the bustling downtown of Amherst. Note that the courthouse is now hidden behind the Post Office and Customhouse, and as yet there are no clocks in the tower. The stacks of lumber, lower right corner, indicate the ongoing construction of Black's stone block, and coupled with that, the arches constructed across Victoria Street, in the vicinity of Havelock and farther east, suggest that the photo was taken in 1887 on the occasion of the Queen's Jubilee. Hickman House and the other structures have yet to commence construction. A fire later that year hastened the construction when those blocks, except Tupper's, were burned out.

Amherst Courthouses, built in 1887 and 1888

PHOTOS AT RIGHT

Shortly after Amherst became the shiretown of Cumberland County in the 1820s, this small, wooden, one-storey Federalist-style courthouse was built as the Inferior Court to deal with local matters. The Supreme Court for the area was located in River Philip. The property had been deeded in trust for township use to Edward Barron, William Black, and Charles Baker by William Freeman in 1783 and it was decided that a courthouse would serve the good of the public. Destroyed by fire in 1887, it was replaced by another in 1888, which remains standing today. Constructed by Rhodes, Curry Company from Amherst red sandstone, the courthouse features classical styling with fan-shaped arches over the first-floor windows and protruding pediments over the second-storey counterparts and the third-floor dormers.

FIRST COUNTY COURTHOUSE, BUILT IN 1840 AND SECOND COURTHOUSE (BELOW), BUILT IN 1888

Post Office

Necessity is often the mother of invention. And so it was with the first Amherst post office, which was established as a matter of convenience in 1810 near the site of the old Fox home on Upper Victoria Street. The location put it in close proximity to the road from Halifax which brought the royal mail coaches. As the town grew, it became obvious a larger facility was needed, and by 1888 a rather austere building was constructed to serve the expanded role of town post office and customs office. This Tudor-Gothic structure, created by Rhodes, Curry Company, was fashioned in a Victorian-Gothic style by architect Thomas Fuller. He is also credited with designing the first House of Commons and the parliamentary library.

Victoria Square

A landmark since 1788, Victoria Square was once known as Courthouse Square but was renamed in 1887 in honour of Queen Victoria's Jubilee. In celebration of the anniversary, the queen donated iron watering troughs to towns throughout the empire, with Amherst receiving two: one was situated at the corner of Church and Albion streets and the other was at Morse's Corner (Victoria and Willow). One of these now sits in Rod MacDougall's backyard at 206 Victoria Street East.

Rhodes Steele Block

A spectacular piece of architecture took form in 1895 when Rhodes, Curry Company completed this project. Designed by H.H. Mott of the Saint John firm of Mott, Myles and Chatwin, it was constructed in the Queen Anne Revival style, evident here in the mixture of wood, brick, and stone in the facade. The third-storey Palladian bay windows are flanked by smaller windows topped with deeply-carved sandstone shells. At street level, consumers of this elaborate structure frequented a grocery store, Wilson's Dress Goods, and P.S. Smith & Son Stationers. W.H. Rogers, a local lawyer, worked from his offices on the west end of the second floor. Steele, a local merchant, was also located here.

Maritime Block

Built in 1907, the Maritime Block on Church Street features ball and pedestal ornamentation on the roof line, and decorative lintels above the second and third-floor windows. The main storefronts of the street-level Martin's and the Palace were traditional, and rather plain by comparison, in design.

Bank of Montreal

The simple lines of this building constructed in 1906 served as the home of the Bank of Montreal. The contractor, James Reid of Sydney, used Amherst red sandstone, while Rhodes, Curry Company supplied and installed the mahogany interior. One feature of merit was the use of Roman arched windows.

Bank of Nova Scotia

PHOTOS AT RIGHT

The Bank of Nova Scotia opened its Amherst branch in 1871, and by 1887 business was thriving to the point where head office staff in Halifax ordered the construction of elegant offices for Amherst's Victoria Street. John R. Hall of Boston designed the Classical Revival facade showcasing fluted Corinthian columns topped with a pair of turrets bedecked with a finial on the roofline. This building was demolished and replaced by the current one in 1907 by the highly-regarded firm of Darling and Pearson, which had been responsible for the Royal Ontario Museum, Trinity College, and the Winnipeg post office. Described as a plain version of the Beaux-Arts Revival style with classical details, plans indicate a balance between intricate old style and Darling and Pearson's preference for colossal order in both design and ornamentation.

BANK OF NOVA SCOTIA IN 1887 (ABOVE) AND CURRENT BANK (BELOW) BUILT IN 1907

ROYAL BANK

Customers first walked between the elaborate Corinthian pillars of the renowned Royal Bank of Canada on Victoria Street in Amherst on Nov. 20, 1906. And they continue to do so today. Situated next to B.W. Baker's brick building on land purchased from George D. Hewson, the building was designed by Howard Stone, an American who moved to Montreal in 1898 where he was appointed architect for the bank. Before his death in 1918, Stone was hailed as "executing some of the most accomplished classical bank designs in the country." Constructed of Amherst red sandstone, the Renaissance-style facade employs a variety of window designs: arched at street level, peaked on the second storey, and rectangular in shape on the third. The first floor housed the bank offices, the second contained the manager's quarters, and the third was used for junior staff. Later, the second floor was turned into the Marshlands Club, where merchants were able to socialize and seek refuge from the stresses of the day.

Town hall and fire station

The first town hall, built in 1888–89 by Rhodes, Curry Company on property vacated by the Roman Catholic Church, housed all civic offices as well as the No. 1 Fire Station on the ground floor. Town hall records show that Amherst was incorporated on December 17, 1889 with the total real estate property and income being $1,824,646, owned by a population of 4,702. After the first town election Thomas Dunlap became the town's first mayor. Councillors of the day were William Read, B.W. Ralston, J.N. Fage, W.J. Hamilton. H. Curry, and J.L. Fillmore. Records show that the group assembled for its first meeting in January 1890 in the courthouse. This, however, was largely a formality since the only business conducted was the motion to adjourn until the next evening. At that second gathering, committees were appointed; W. F. Donkin was elected town clerk and treasurer and Amherst became a duly incorporated town. *The Amherst Gazette*, in commenting on the election in the following issue, closed its comments by saying, "We have now a town government, each member of which enters upon his duties with a conscientious desire to serve our interests fairly, and to do justice to all, and we trust that our citizens will assist in making the departure conducive to the town's prosperity."

HAVELOCK STREET, C. 1915

This photo shows the side of the Royal Bank on Havelock Street; the front was on Victoria Street. Judging from the maze of electrical, telephone, and telegraph wires, this photograph was taken some time after the turn of the century. The Daily Telegram sign painted on the side of the brick building (still in place) was no indication that the short-lived printing and publishing business run by Claude del Black was still in existence. The paper folded around 1904-05, but the sign was still there in the 1930s and 40s. Tennant's Bottling Works, a.k.a. The Amherst Mineral Water Company, was directly across the street from the printing house.

Chapter 2

Historic Homes

177 VICTORIA STREET EAST

A town known for its towers and turrets is justifiably proud of the architecture that in part defines it. One of the most impressive turn-of-the-century homes in Amherst is the lovely "Victoria," so named for its location on Victoria Street East and the Victorian style of architecture it employs. Designed by Boston architect and watercolour artist Willard R. Mitchell in 1900 for brothers Edgar and Harvey Hewson, the home is considered one of the finest examples of the Queen Anne Revival style of architecture in Canada. No less than the Parks Canada publication, *The Buildings of Canada*, features this residence as its Queen Anne Revival style illustration. It was prominent builder C.J. Silliker who was awarded the contract to build the house for local barrister and businessman Edgar Hewson and his wife Helen in 1907. When complete, it showcased curb-appeal features such as towers, Palladian windows, a steeply-pitched hip roof, and a combination of building materials such as wood, stone, and brick. The combination of all makes the well-maintained Victoria one of the most admired homes in the area.

188 Victoria Street East, c. 1905

While honeymooning in California, Harvey Hewson had this home built just a stone's throw away from his brother's home at 177 Victoria. It is constructed primarily of red sandstone, a building material taken from a quarry east of Willow Street that was opened on property owned by James Donalds—a local cattleman who made his fortune shipping cattle to market by rail—and John McKeen, manager of the Bank of Nova Scotia. The structure reflects the French Romanesque Revival style which had been popularized by the American architect H.H. Richardson in the mid-1800s. Among its many features are a gracious arched entry and porte cochère at the back, elegant details that show little expense was spared by the owner, one of Amherst's wealthiest industrialists, who named the property Beau Sejour.

23 Spring Street

A massive front porch dominated by a pair of two-storey pillars and curved glass bay windows are the defining features of John A. Law's home at 23 Spring Street. It was said to have been built in 1907 for $3,000.

155 Victoria Street East

Constructed in 1870 by Robert McCully, a prominent local lawyer who also served as the first president of Amherst Boot and Shoe, this home sits atop a sloping property that provides a spectacular view of Victoria Street East. Architectural details include the curved lines of onion-like caps over symmetrical bay windows and a keyhole verandah entry that welcomes visitors. Known as the Bank of Montreal home, it was so named after the bank bought it from the McCullys with the intent that it be occupied by the branch manager while that person worked in Amherst. This was not an unusual arrangement at the time; a nearby property at 192 Victoria Street East is known as the Bank of Nova Scotia home for similar reasons.

Grove Cottage

Now the home of the Cumberland County Museum, this photograph taken in November 1929 shows the house which is believed to have been built by Robert McGowan Dickey. However, it is perhaps best known as the residence of his son, Robert Barry Dickey, a Canadian senator who was one of Amherst's four fathers of Confederation. Built circa 1838, the house was originally constructed according to a floor plan that was popular at the time: each floor has a central hallway with two rooms on each side. In total, the one-and-a-half-storey house has a modest eight rooms and a small back ell for the kitchen and servants' quarters. When R.B. inherited the estate from his father in 1854, he was established as a lawyer and required space for a new office. Consequently, a large room on the north side was built. Since this made the building lopsided, three small dormers were added across the front of the house to provide balance to the building. Later, James A. Dickey, a former mayor of Amherst, altered the house again by adding a covered verandah, a large late-Victorian newel post in the foyer, and his monogram on the front door.

CHARLES R. SMITH HOME

TOP LEFT

This sprawling home stood at 2 Lawrence Street and was owned by Charles R. Smith, a lawyer with interests in several local industries and a member of both the golf club and the Marshlands Club. The house stood next to the church on what was known locally as Smith's Corner. Smith donated the church land and the next building down was the office building of R.K. Smith, son of Charles, which is now the home of Cumberland Publishing.

N.A. RHODES HOME

TOP RIGHT

A successful entrepreneur and the founder of Rhodes, Curry Company, N.A. Rhodes built this home at 57 Havelock Street in 1890. Across the street to the south, he constructed a large multi-family housing complex for his employees.

JAMES EDWARD LUSBY HOME

BOTTOM LEFT

James Edward Lusby, a local mason known as Jim Ed and recognized as securing Amherst's first street paving contract for $2,498, owned this charming home at 53 West Victoria Street. Its distinguishing keyhole theme is seen in the front verandah styled in what is known as a Carpenter's Gothic design. The style appears in a pair of windows and an interior archway. One of the more interesting early features of the house was a rope-pulled elevator, which was used to ferry fuel from the basement to the upper floors.

J.B. LUSBY HOME

BOTTOM RIGHT

Josiah Black Lusby, a farmer, included a trio of classical two-storey pillars in the facade of this home built in 1910 at 196 Victoria Street East. He constructed the home on the first and second lots of land purchased from A. William Black. A noticeable feature is the circular window set in the centre. Lusby sold the property in 1929 to George Minchin Barker of Two Barkers. While the property once served as a bed-and-breakfast, it has since reverted to a single-family residence.

Amos Pugsley's House

This home, constructed by local farmer Amos Pugsley in 1873, is a good example of the Victorian style of architecture, which is based primarily on the Gothic conception. Situated on the north side of Victoria Street West, it features a corner tower—a popular architectural addition in the Queen Anne Revival period—and a high-pitched gable that breaks the eaveline in a triangular hood fashion. Centrally, a dormer with two windows provides additional architectural interest.

David W. Robb House

David W. Robb built this home for his family at 98 Church Street around 1885. In 1890, he became president and chief engineer in the company founded by his father, Alexander Robb. At one point, the home was remodeled and the distinctive square tower and tall chimney removed.

Dickey House

An excellent example of Second Empire architecture (popular from 1870 to 1900), the house at 169 Victoria Street East sets forth a steeply-pitched Mansard roof, square in shape, and shows heavy bracketing that is Italianate in origin. Chimneys are discreetly placed so as not to interrupt the street front views of the corner property, which was once the home of Senator Arthur Dickey. Son of R.B. Dickey, he held a trio of federal cabinet portfolios between 1881 and 1901. They included secretary of state and ministry of militia, defense, and justice.

Spring Street

In the forefront of this photo is the large home of commercial traveller W.B. Murdoch. It features a broad verandah, delicate stained glass windows, and a widow's walk. The central home was owned by photographer Carl Pridham, who may be credited with documenting much of Amherst's architectural and social history. The photographer had a studio on Station Street near the Opera House and later moved the business to Church Street where it was purchased by Edgar P. Smith and operated by his sons R.H. and R.P. Smith. The company was later sold to Harry Pridham, a cousin of the original owner. In the background is a home owned by John Crosman that even today showcases a wonderful carved gable around its third-storey Palladian window. Mr. Crosman was a manager at Amherst Foundry Company.

VICTORIA STREET WEST

Known as Victoria Street West, this rutted and unpaved route crossing the railway into the downtown core was a main thoroughfare for early local residents who trod along the plank sidewalks. The introduction of automobiles in the early 1900s led to the need to improve road and sidewalk conditions, and by 1910, the last of these plank walkways were removed. Visible in the background of this photograph is 9 Victoria Street West, with its unusual square turret bedecked with an onion-like roof. The attractive architecture belonged to Titus Lowther in its early years. Closer to the forefront of the picture are the addresses of 15 and 17 Victoria Street West, which also showcase turrets topped with the decorative finials that were so popular at the turn of the century.

Chapter 3

Business and Industry

AMHERST EVENING NEWS, C. 1894

Amherst readers enjoyed a number of local newspapers during the late 1800s when debates of the day were found on the pages of many town papers. Making its foray into business in the late 1860s under J. Albert Black was *The Amherst Gazette*, the first newspaper in the town. The second—*The Maritime Sentinel*—surfaced in the 1870s and was taken over by B.W. Baker when it became mired in financial problems. He, in turn, later sold the plant to the *Amherst Daily News*, established in 1893. Here, editor and owner of *Amherst Evening News* J.H. Froggart and his family pose for a Christmas photograph. *The Press* was another pioneer daily in 1890, but again, financial difficulties struck and it was taken over by the *News*. *The Daily Telegram* and *Daily News* also perished after short careers.

Amherst Boot and Shoe Factory

The year 1867 was an historic one for Amherst. Not only did it mark Confederation, but Amherst Boot and Shoe Factory opened in the general prosperity of the times. Incorporated by special act of the Nova Scotia Legislature on May 7, the company's incorporators were E.S. Crafts, Robert McCully, William M. Sleep, Thomas R. Black, Fred W. Bent, R.B. Huestis, D.F. Quigley, W.M. Fullerton, Atcheson Moffatt, Eliakim Newcombe, R.B. Dickey, Jonathan McCully, H.G. Pineo, and Charles Tupper. Subsequently, the Steam Tanning Company was organized and managed by C.R. Casey at the same time that the firm of Pride and Quigley was doing a large and profitable boot and shoe business in Amherst.

By 1876, the three companies had amalgamated as Amherst Boot, Shoe, and Tanning Company and began the manufacture of boots and shoes on an increased scale in Moffatt's Block. Within a year, the output was $66,154 although an unfortunate fire at the tannery that year cost the company, which carried no insurance on that portion, some $12,000. After surviving another fire and the Depression, the tanning branch was resold to Casey, and in 1879 confident directors built a new three-storey brick building at the rear of Moffat's Block, complete with warehouses and engine house. By 1885, another new factory and warerooms were built on the corner of Station Street and Crescent Avenue and by 1907, when output was recorded at $838,138, still another new factory was constructed. A group of Saint John businessmen bought the company in 1906, but it returned to local hands in 1908.

In 1911, the Halifax branch was flourishing, the Amherst plant was being extended, and a market was growing in the west with a distribution centre being opened in Regina to help keep pace with demand. Not surprisingly, revenues surpassed $1 million in 1916. Production and sales were upheld by war and early post-war demands until the latter part of the 1920s. But once the Depression hit in 1921, sales fell, production was cut, and losses were tallied. By 1927, the company was forced to close, marking a sad end to a business that initially prided itself on its shares being held by all classes of local citizens.

AMHERST FOUNDRY

In 1890, J.A. Crossman and J.A. Laws began casting mill and machinery supplies. By the following year, they were casting stoves and hollowware and had hired four men to work alongside their original employee, E.S. Palmer. Early investors in the company included William Knight, Avard Black, Charles A. Lusby, and Charles A. Black. The early 1900s saw the company continue to grow. In 1901, some forty men were employed at the business; by 1902, a new brick building was added on Douglas Avenue; by 1903, the company was incorporated; by 1904, a new plant for the manufacture of enamelled sanitary ware was added; and by 1906, a joint stock company was formed. Large additions were made to the moulding shop and the capacity of the enamelling department was doubled. In 1913, 120 men were working at a plant consisting of a moulding shop, fitting shop, enamelling building, mill and pattern shop, all constructed of brick and stone. Consumers throughout Canada and Bermuda purchased from a line of stoves and ranges (including the Cumberland Hot Air Furnace) and a line of Beaver Brand cast iron enameled sanitary ware including bathtubs, lavatories, and sinks. For a time, these products were showcased in a large retail department on Victoria Street in Amherst. In 1928, the company merged with Fawcett of Sackville, New Brunswick under the name of Enamel and Heating Products Limited.

WORKERS POSING IN FRONT OF WASHTUB MOULDS.

Amherst Harbour and Wharf

Situated at the mouth of the LaPlanche River, Amherst Harbour was declared a port by proclamation on April 3, 1907. But it was as early as June 1903 that a contract had been let, with a pile wharf completed in late 1904 and a spur line from the Intercolonial Railway mainline completed in September 1906. By November of that year, business was said to be flourishing and increasing so fast that more derricks and machinery were needed so that more ships could unload at one time. As 1908 ended, there were two piers with more than 1,200 feet of wharf frontage. Soon, two range lights were constructed near the entrance, new freight houses were erected, and a thorough hydrographical survey of Cumberland Basin completed. The Public Works department also completed an Amherst Point wharf and ferry slips at Amherst Point and Minudie.

AMHERST PIANO WORKS LIMITED

Piano retailer J.A. MacDonald had a dream. With $500,000, he saw it realized when he capitalized Amherst Pianos Limited in 1912 by establishing his business in conjunction with the small H.A. Hillcoat Company of Amherst. The union took place in 1913 in temporary quarters in the Malleable Iron Foundry building until a new brick factory was ready. Located on Sackville Road, it rose three storeys and measured 220 feet by 60 feet. Quality products featuring hand-carved details such as pilasters and piano legs were lovingly churned out by a master carver who spent a month each year in Amherst preparing inventory from local spruce, birch, and maple.

Business was brisk, with principal markets being Canada and the West Indies. By 1913, one hundred men worked at the factory which produced player pianos that cost $750. World War One brought some disruption, but after it ended, the former Maple Leaf Hotel in Amherst was renovated to handle production of the Cremonaphone Talking Machine.

Amherst Pianos was said to be at its peak in 1924, shipping a carload of pianos a week, but came to a halt by 1928 when Manufacturers' Finance Corporation, which backed it, failed. Suddenly, demand decreased while freight rates, competition, and the popularity of radio all increased. Here, employees pose outside the factory that produced pianos, which today continue to make music.

Amherst Red Sandstone Company

Sandstone has been the predominant building stone quarried in Nova Scotia over the last two hundred years. Buff, olive, and tan-coloured, it was readily available in Amherst and Wallace in Cumberland County as well as near Pictou and New Glasgow in Pictou County, and Tatamagouche in Colchester County. Several historically important buildings in the region, including the Halifax Armouries, were constructed of Amherst's famous red sandstone.

Coady's Livery Stables

TOP RIGHT

This flourishing business in the early 1900s was located on LaPlanche Street near where the current law office of Hicks LeMoine is situated. It formed the taxi company of the day, with owner John Coady in a top hat using this carriage for occasions such as weddings, funerals, and important civic events.

Amherst Winter Fair

BOTTOM RIGHT

Held in Amherst since 1901, the Maritime Winter Fair was among the largest of livestock shows in Canada, second only to the Royal Winter Fair in Toronto. It was said to be directly responsible for agricultural breeding advancements among Maritime cattle, horses, sheep, swine, and foxes.

COADY'S LIVERY STABLES (RIGHT) AND MARITIME WINTER FAIR SITE (BELOW)

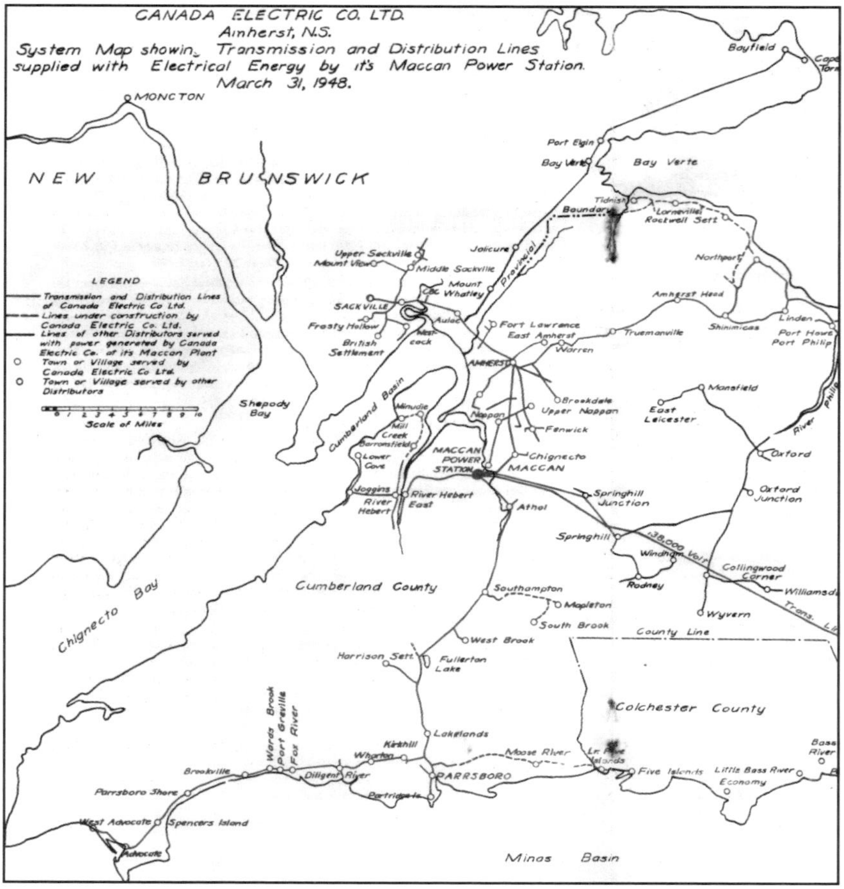

CANADA ELECTRIC COMPANY

Amherstonians saw the light in 1889 when the Canada Electric Company was formed under directors D.W. Robb and N.A. Rhodes. The first plant, with a capacity of 150 horsepower, was located on Electric Street, opened purposely to house the light plant. At about the same time, the Coffy Hotel was moved from Victoria Street to Electric Street and made over into tenements. The charge was based on the number of lights used and on their locations: drawing room—3 cents; lower halls—7 cents; kitchens—5 cents. By 1906, the Standard Engineering Company installed a 500-horsepower engine at Chignecto, followed by another in 1907, giving a capacity of 1000 horsepower to Amherst industries while the Canada Electric Company supplied the power for lighting. At first, the power came on at dusk and was shut off at midnight. Around 1889–1890, the power was left on all night and by 1909, the power for approximately 8000 lights was supplied. In 1911, the companies merged under the name of the Canada Electric Company Limited to supply lights and power to Amherst and other areas of Cumberland County.

DOUGLAS & COMPANY HARDWARE

TOP RIGHT

By the time it celebrated a century in business, this hardware firm was among the oldest in the Maritimes. Besides local service, it catered to a wholesale market in the Maritime provinces. The business was established by Benjamin Douglas and carried on by his son D.W. Douglas, who was succeeded by J.H. Douglas.

DOUGLAS & COMPANY HARDWARE

DOUGLAS, ROGERS COMPANY LIMITED

Well known for its fire, automobile, casualty, marine, and boiler insurance, the firm of Douglas Rogers was organized in 1900 by Hon. J. Robson Douglas.

Christie Trunk & Bag Company Limited

"Best going—best returning" was the slogan of the quality luggage the Christie family manufactured and sold in a marketplace that included Canada, as well as a thriving export trade with the British West Indies and some parts in South America. The business began in 1863 when three of five Christie brothers—Charles, George, and Alex—moved from River Hebert to became partners in Christie Brothers and establish a carriage factory and woodworking mill at 71 Albion Street, next to the home of Charles I. Christie. Later, they expanded into making caskets, offering funeral services, manufacturing luggage, and opening a swimming and bathing house located at the lower end of the building near the culvert that drained Christie Pond. By 1891, this poster had been printed advertising a 50 foot by 20 foot swimming tank "affording excellent opportunities for learning the art of swimming," with water and bathrooms heated by steam and fitted with hot and cold shower baths. Tuesday and Friday afternoons were reserved for ladies only. Season tickets could be purchased by applying at the office.

Meanwhile, the business of making caskets and luggage was carried on as one industry until February 1913 when the casket portion of the industry was sold to a Toronto firm, Dominion Manufacturers (though it continued to operate from the same building). In 1893, the Christies continued to manufacture luggage under the name of Christie Trunk & Bag, eventually relying on warehouses in Winnipeg and Toronto for storage of the finished product.

A March 12, 1918 article in the *Amherst Gazette* notes that "whether it was grinding grain, building carriages and sleighs, preparing the last resting place for our silent dead, or manufacturing trunks, suitcases, travelling bags, the name of Christie always stood for honesty, integrity and worth."

Staff of Christie Trunk & Bag Company Limited and Dominion Manufacturers Limited, 1934

Front row, l-r: Frank Turner, Jim Simmons, Charlie Simmons, Gerry Dupuis, Eva Landry, Harvey Dobson, Blair Davison, Gren Kellegrew, Tannis Girouard, A.P. Harlow, and Percy Sargeant.

Second row, l-r: Dan Rushton, Harry Bell, Joe O'Blenis, Earl Thurston, Herbie Lorette, Fred Landry, Charlie Connolly, unidentified, Ernest Landry, Joe Durant, Fred Estabrooks, George White, Ray Kellegrew, John Simmons, and Wil Carty.

Back row, l-r: Joe Burke, C.B. Christie, John Chisholm, Harry Keith, Gerald Legere, Ray Simmons, Rolly Simmons, Leonard Simmons, Alfie Burke, and Stephen Durant. Temple Mills is shown standing in the doorway.

DUNLAPS Thomas Dunlap came to Amherst from Truro in 1865 to open a general store dealing in hardware dry goods, boots, shoes, and clothing. Later, his brother Henry Dunlap and William A. McDonald also became associated with him and the firm operated as Dunlap Brothers and Company. In 1884, a tailoring department was opened at the back of the store and operated by Fred Fowler. The name of the company was again changed, becoming known as Dunlap, Fowler and Company.

Soon, George W. Cook, a Maritime fur specialist, joined the company under Dunlap, Cook and Company. Occupying the greater portion of the three-storey Treen Block, the firm flourished and business prospered. In 1901, they employed a staff of more than fifty operators, with another fifteen to twenty during the busy season. Nine years later, they were employing about two hundred men during the height of annual production.

A tailor shop on the north side of Victoria Street resulted as part of that business. In this group photograph taken between 1886 and 1888, the following are identified: Margaret Dickie of Mount Pleasant, Elizabeth Sarson (wearing a locket) of Pugwash, Laura Dowlan, and Hannah McEachern (née Fraser).

HEWSON WOOLEN MILLS

Two innovative brothers are responsible for organizing one of Amherst's great industries, Hewson Woolen Mills. H.L. and E.E. Hewson began the enterprise in September 1902 from West Pleasant Street by the main line of the Intercolonial Railway. Measuring 600 feet by 150 feet, the brick and stone structure was equipped with modern equipment that enabled it to spin native and foreign wools into products that retailed across Canada. By 1905, the plant employed one hundred people and by 1906 or 1907, a knitting factory was added to keep pace with demand. Ill health contributed to the Hewsons' relinquishing management of the mills, which continued to operate as Amherst Woolen Mills Limited under Colonel John Stanfield. In 1911, when Frank Stanfield was made president, the mill was using four hundred thousand pounds of wool annually; a large portion of this came from the Maritimes, with the remainder being brought in from foreign countries such as Australia. Some two-thirds of the plant's output was going to western Canada by the following year when a three-storey wing and new machinery were added to the operation, which by then employed 225 men.

McKay Cars and Road Transportation

Famous in its day as a racer and for a cross-Canada tour, the fabled McKay car of Amherst—with its hand-buffed leather upholstery and electric self-starter—was one of the first automobiles in the country. But the parent company, the Nova Scotia Carriage Company, actually began operation in 1868 in Kentville. It prospered until just after the turn of the century, when automobiles began to appear on provincial roads and by 1908, the original owners ceased production and rented the factory to Prince Edward Island natives Jack and Dan McKay. The duo continued to make carriages and sleighs before deciding the time had come to manufacture automobiles. With no experience in the relatively new automotive field but plenty of financing, the McKays literally learned how to make cars from the wheels up. According to local history, the head mechanic in the McKay factory learned his trade by taking an Oldsmobile apart and putting it together again.

By 1910, 25 McKay cars had been assembled in the Kentville plant. Once the company moved to Amherst, another 100 cars, such as this one owned by A.G. Robb (photo at right), were produced between 1911 and 1914.

If the McKay helped usher in a new era of transportation, it also brought about an inevitable clash with horsepower. Roads of the time were poor and farmers complained vociferously that inconsiderate drivers speeding along in the noisy, newfangled contraptions were spooking horses on the way to markets or work fields. Conscious of the brewing discontent, the County Council of Cumberland in 1909 restricted cars to travel in the area only five days a week, except on the Tyndal Roads where motorists were free to travel seven days a week. According to the same law, when a car met a horse and rider on the road, the motorist was to give them the right of way and offer assistance if the car frightened the animal in any way.

The number of cars produced in Amherst fell far short of the one thousand the company had hoped would take to the road. Still, the future looked bright at the time: a prospectus released in 1912 spoke of a $2-million investment, there were predictions of a payroll with 1,500 employees, and a quadrupling of production. When the province published an industrial review in 1913, the Nova Scotia Carriage and Motor Car Company of Amherst received a glowing report. "The product (of the company) comprises automobiles, auto trucks, carriages, and sleighs. One hundred and twenty-five men are presently employed. Nova Scotia wood and steel are largely (used). When present extensions are completed the output will amount in value to one million dollars annually."

A.G. ROBB AT 'THE SPRING."

However, a year after it was featured in the industrial review, the company was bankrupt. Operations ceased late in 1914 with the onset of World War One, a shortage of operating capital, and a failure to meet the demands of the motoring public contributing to its sudden demise.

Maritime Pant Manufacturing Company Limited

As it did for so many Amherst industries, World War Two provided a great economic boost to Maritime Pant Manufacturing Company Limited. Under contract to the Department of National Defence, the company turned out nearly two million garments for the armed forces. By 1941, the company had the resources to buy a four-storey building on Douglas Avenue, which it converted to civilian work at the end of the war.

Moss Jewellers

Myer Moss saw Canada as the land of opportunity. Immigrating from England in the 1850s, he set up business first in Halifax and later in Pictou. His son, George L. Moss, is believed to have established a shop in Amherst around 1881 just as the area's economy was beginning to thrive. First located on Victoria Street where the Royal Bank now sits, the business—which once housed the town's butcher shop—moved to its permanent location at 91 Victoria Street in 1903.

AMHERST LIVERY STABLE

MUNSIE'S LIVERY STABLE

Amherst Livery Stable later became Munsie's Livery Stable, then Amherst Fishmarket, which was owned by A.P. McKinnon.

Rhodes, Curry Company

How did Rhodes, Curry Company grow from one of the ubiquitous sash-and-door factories sprinkled throughout the Maritimes into one of the largest industrial plants in the region?

The story begins with Nelson A. Rhodes (born in Amherst in 1845) and Nathaniel Curry (born in Cornwallis in 1851), both of whom became apprenticed carpenters and moved separately to the United States as young journeymen carpenters. The two might never have met, except that at some point, Rhodes met Sarah, who was Curry's sister, and the two married. The three travelled to Amherst in 1876–1877 and it was there that the seeds of a business idea were sown. It is likely that even they could not have foreseen that their company would change the appearance of the Maritimes through the sheer number of buildings it erected and through the composition of some imposing public structures.

Initially, the men established a business with a man named Bayard Dodge. The partnership was dismantled after the business was burned out and Dodge left for Boston. Left by themselves, Rhodes and Curry rebuilt the sash-and-door factory only to see it destroyed by another fire two years later. Again, they rebuilt, aided by a number of town citizens, a fact that Rhodes never forgot. After consolidating their debts and securing financing from private investors (a common practice in the days before banks and building societies were firmly established), the business prospered, propelled in no small manner by a thriving economy.

By 1893, Rhodes Curry became a joint stock company, incorporated as Rhodes, Curry & Company Limited. It also expanded into the railway business by purchasing the Saint John based J. Harris Car Works and moving the operation to Amherst. The company had a plant in Sydney and, as its banking became too large for then-existing facilities in Halifax, the Bank of Montreal established branches in Amherst and Halifax, principally at the beginning to meet the company's requirements. With an expected life span of 10 years, rebuilding wooden freight and coal cars for the expanding railway system of Canada provided a strong market for Rhodes, Curry Company. As an employer of 350 people, the company built 1,200 freight cars and 15 passenger coaches between 1893 and 1895. Such activity had a ripple effect since it supplied a brisk trade at the local docks where the wood for construction was delivered by schooner. Various records note that there would be as many as three to four large ships at the wharf at any one time.

The first cracks in this relative prosperity began to show in 1909, the year that Nelson Rhodes died. Rhodes, Curry amalgamated with Montreal's Canada Car Company and Dominion Car & Foundry Company Limited, also of Montreal, and became known as Canada Car and Foundry Company. Many Amherstonians went on to rue the day because the car company never met the production levels of the woodworking factory and was eventually forced to close. Still, at the time, Nathaniel Curry, who was named president of the new company and moved to Montreal to oversee the new group, expressed optimism for a prosperous future: "The present capacity of these combined works is sufficient to take care of the Canadian railways for several years to come," he told those at the inauguration. "During the present year, we will turn out 12,000 cars, even if we should book no further orders. Of this number, 4,000 have already been delivered. The value of the Canadian Car & Foundry Company's output from its three plants amount to $1,200,000 per month."

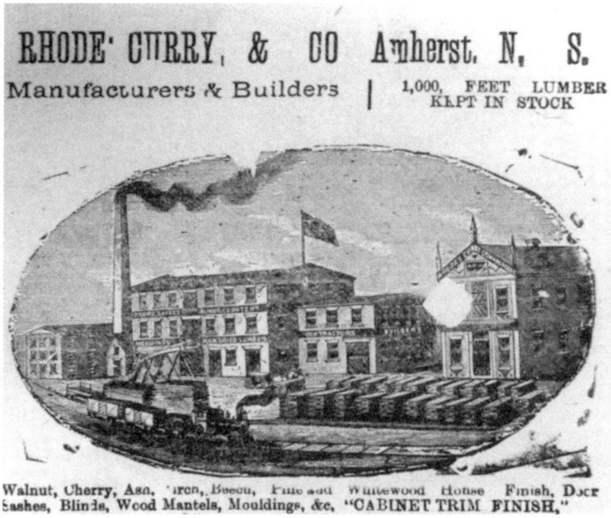

The earliest passenger cars produced by this company continued designs such as the Pullman Company's all-wood cars for the Grand Trunk and Grand Trunk Pacific with vestibules and double windows having arched upper sashes. Canadian Northern passenger car orders also came in 1910, when 10 sleepers, five baggage, and four dining cars were built for that road. In 1913, 15 wooden tourist cars and 20 wooden baggage cars were also built. Records show that the company built 28 cars for the Intercolonial, 181 cars for the Grand Trunk, 206 cars for the Grand Trunk Pacific, 122 cars for the Canadian Northern, 866 cars for the Canadian Pacific, and 1254 cars for the Canadian National. The first steel tank cars built in Canada were constructed at this plant, along with the first steel frame box cars and the first steel twin pocket hopper cars.

By 1918 when the Allies broke through the Western Front and World War One was drawing to a close, the factory was pressed into overtime producing shells and transports to be used in the final push. When war was declared in 1939, the factory became extremely busy again as cars on the assembly line were replaced by airplanes. Avro Ansons were constructed and Hawker Hurricanes repaired at the site. Times were good.

With the end of World War Two, however, this prosperity disappeared virtually overnight. The Amherst plant, after being only on sporadic production since 1919, was finally closed entirely in 1931. The building construction part of the company continued until 1919, when it was organized as a separate entity that continued operation on a much-reduced scale until it finally closed in the 1950s. The legacy it left was large and is evident even today in thousands of buildings that dot the Atlantic Provinces.

Robb Engineering Limited

In 1836, a small boy arrived in Amherst to serve an apprenticeship with Amos Page, whose workshop on the northeast corner of Victoria and Eddy streets was at the industrial centre of the village. Page made and repaired everything from silverware, watches, and clocks to tinware. By 1848, that apprentice, twenty-one year-old Alexander Robb, decided to open his own shop with fellow apprentice Frederick Bulmer in a small space at or near the site of the Etter and Pugsley store. After a year or so, Bulmer moved to Antigonish and started a similar business in stoves and tinware while Robb continued plying his trade in Amherst.

Around the same time, the first cast iron cooking stoves were being imported from the United States by Amos Seaman, known as King Seaman of Minudie. Not finding a ready market for the new-fangled stoves, he turned them over to his friend Robb, who distributed them through his agents in Cumberland and Westmorland counties. From that inauspicious start, Robb nurtured a large business in stoves, which he thereafter imported directly from the United States on schooners. The period of the American Civil War (1861–1865) proved particularly favourable for such importations because of the heavy discount on American currency. One Canadian dollar was worth about two U.S. dollars.

By war's end, Robb decided to build an iron foundry for the production of stoves and other similar products. The first cast in Robb's Foundry was made in August 1865, overseen by some 25 employees. The output amounted to about $30,000 a year. This was no small accomplishment for the time, considering the difficulties experienced in transportation. Every pound of pig iron, moulding sand, anthracite coal for melting, and other raw materials had to be imported by water, landed on the mudflats at Fort Lawrence or elsewhere, and trucked to the works. With navigation closed in winter, it was necessary to lay in heavy stocks before the snow fell. A machine shop and foundry were added in the following year to supply the demands of the coal mines and lumber mills in the surrounding country.

As business increased and Robb's health began to fail, his sons David and Fred joined the firm, with the former filling the position of president and chief engineer and the latter becoming the company secretary and treasurer. At this point, the name was changed to A. Robb and Sons, a name it would keep until 1890 or 1891 when the company incorporated and became known as Robb Armstrong Engineering: Electric Lighting and Tramways. Around the same time, the family mourned the death of Alexander Robb, who passed away early in 1891, the same year that A.G. Robb returned from the Massachusetts Institute of Technology where he was studying mechanical engineering and began designing engines. He later became chief engineer for the company.

ALEXANDER ROBB

By 1894, Robb's had outgrown the old premises and had built a new, more modern plant with the capability of producing engines of up to 300 horsepower. Sadly, Fred Robb, after twenty-three years of successful business management, drowned in 1897 at the YMCA Boys' Camp at Fox Harbour. His brother, D.W., continued the management until his retirement in 1920. Robb engines were supplied to almost every part of the world until the advent of hydroelectric power and steam turbines supplemented the reciprocating engine and the company sought other lines of manufacture. During the war, Robb's was among the largest producers of shells and marine engines for the British, Canadian, American, and French governments.

Pugsley's Drug Store

Sir Charles Tupper, one of the fathers of Confederation, wanted to serve his community further and spend more time at his medical practice. The best solution, as he saw it, was to open a drugstore. Pugsley's Drug Store, as it is now known, has been in the same location, although in different structures, since 1843 when it first began serving customers.

In 1851, finding that his profession and an increasing interest in the provincial political arena were forcing a restructuring of priorities, Tupper relinquished his interest in the drugstore to his brother, Nathan, who was also a doctor. Employed in the store was R.C. Fuller of England who, in 1875, obtained Nathan Tupper's shares in the business; the store then became known as R.C. Fuller and Company. In 1882, John W. Morrison, an apprentice at the store, attended the Philadelphia College of Pharmacy, graduating as the gold medal winner of his class. He became a partner with Fuller a decade later, around the time the present store was built. In 1889, the store was put into a new building called the Tupper Block, where it has remained ever since.

In 1926, B.T. Pugsley entered the firm after having graduated from the Maritime College of Pharmacy at Dalhousie University in Halifax. When Fuller died in 1936, Pugsley entered into a partnership with Morrison. Following the latter's death in 1948, Pugsley purchased full control of the firm and the store name was changed to Pugsley's Pharmacy.

STANFIELDS Charles E. Stanfield had no idea when he immigrated to America in 1855 that he would found the firm that is known as a leader in its field today. Along with his brother-in-law, Samuel E. Dawson, Stanfield founded the Tryon Woolen Mills in Tryon, Prince Edward Island in 1856, ultimately selling out to his partner a decade later. Not one to sit idle, he went on to open the Truro Woolen Mills in 1870, then the St. Croix Woolen Mills, The Union Woolen Mills at Farnham, and Truro Felt Works.

Known as a creative genius, Charles constantly developed new equipment and new products such as the first cardigan jackets and stockinettes in Canada, heavy rib underwear, and the famous "drop seat." He also manufactured sweater cloth and knitting yarn. In 1916, Stanfield's Limited became associated with Amherst when it bought out the Hewson Woollen Mills, which had closed in 1914 due to financial complications and reopened as Amherst Woolen Mills, employing 130 men.

This mill manufactured up to 1,500 yards of cloth per day during World War One, producing fine wool blankets, knitting yarns, and cloth. By 1919, the workers joined the general strike in Amherst in May and June and were among the last in the town to return to work. War and early post-war orders kept the plant operating, although it was shut down for a while during the depression of 1921. In 1923, the plant was finally shut down and abandoned.

TINGLEY MONUMENTS

The year was 1846. In the United States, Texas joined the union as the 28th state, the Mexican-American War started, and baseball began to be played regularly. In Europe, the Irish potato famine led to starvation and mass emigration. In British North America, Upper Canada and Lower Canada had recently joined together as a British colony, but Canada would only be formed twenty-one years later. It was also the year that John C. Tingley established Tingley Granite Works at Hopewell Cape, New Brunswick, beginning a business that would become the oldest monument manufacturing plant in the country. Trained in the trade of stone carving, a skill the family brought with them when they immigrated to New England in the 1600s and later to New Brunswick with the United Empire Loyalists, Tingley began a tradition that continues today in Amherst, where the company relocated in 1917 following a disastrous fire. The town was chosen because of its central location. As the material of choice evolved from marble to granite with the development of harder tools at the turn of the century, raw granite was imported by Tingleys from Sweden, Finland, the United States, and Canada. Today, the company continues a proud tradition into the millennium.

Two Barkers

At Barkers, the system for transporting cash and receipts to and from the cashier incorporated a system of high-speed cords running over pulleys along a small track just below the ceiling. Each counter location was equipped with a vertical sidetrack between the counter and the main pulley line above. With a continuously running pulley line, there was always an incoming and an outgoing line at each counter station.

The clerk placed the cash and an invoice for the merchandise in a small metal box that ran on the track and had a device that clamped the box onto the running cord. When the box was engaged, it was picked up by the cord and carried along the track to the cashier terminal on the mezzanine floor. The cashier removed the box, made change, and added a receipt for the merchandise, then re-engaged the box to the outgoing side of the cord. Diversion stitches built into the boxes for each counter station ensured that the returning box would be diverted down the sidetrack from the main cord line to the appropriate counter station, where it would automatically disengage from the running cord. The clerk gave the customer the change and receipt, and the transaction was completed. A single cashier could handle a multitude of sales originating throughout the store, and at peak periods, another cashier could be employed.

G.M. BARKER LIMITED

The entrepreneurial spirit of the Barkers extended beyond their department store. Under the name G.M. Barker Limited, Chevrolet cars were sold from a property next door to Two Barkers (now known as Jacob's Larder). This photograph shows the Barker business, which serviced cars from a neighbouring property in the rear parking lot of the department store.

Taylor and Tennants

Amherst Spring Ginger Beer, Iron Brew and Nectar Nerve Food were all manufactured by the Amherst Mineral Spring Company, which was started about 1880 on Havelock Street. In 1890 or 1891, the plant was purchased by Taylor and Tennant, who had started a bottling business in 1886. By 1894, when they had moved to a larger building with more modern machinery, the company was manufacturing about 20 varieties of temperance drinks as well as fruit syrup.

CUTTING ICE ON EMBREE'S POND

In the days before electrical refrigeration, the cutting and marketing of ice was an important industry. Its success depended, to a large extent, on the amount found on Embree's Pond where, depending on the weather, work would begin after Christmas and last until February. Prices varied, but blocks of ice generally retailed for around three cents per ten pounds. As with so many industries of the time, horses were integral to the ice business. They were first pressed into use to tow ploughs and clear the pond's frozen surface of snow. Then, they would haul the ice blocks, from designated cut areas on the pond called sets, to storage. Far from being routine, this process was often fraught with stress since it was not uncommon for the horses to fall into the water and drown. A fallen horse would naturally panic, so a noose would be thrown around its neck and tightened until the animal lost consciousness, thereby allowing it to be pulled to safety. Fortunately, motor-driven saws and tractors eventually replaced this traditional method of cutting ice.

Chapter 4

Public and Professional Life

SIR CHARLES TUPPER'S LAST VISIT TO AMHERST, 1913

Sir Charles Tupper, a native of Amherst and a father of Confederation, paid his last visit to the town in 1913. Schoolchildren lined Victoria Street up to Havelock, each waving a Union Jack flag in greeting.

Lord Jeffrey Amherst

The man for whom the Town of Amherst is named was born on January 29, 1717 at Riverhead, Kent, England. Ironically, this little-known supply colonel had never been to North America before he was promoted to major general and arrived at Halifax in 1758 to lead the final siege of Louisbourg. Under his leadership, Ticonderoga was captured, followed by Montreal in 1760. In 1768, Amherst refused the appointment of Governor of Virginia only to accept the position of Governor of Guernsey two years later. From 1772 to 1795, he served as commander-in-chief to the forces and was military advisor to the British government during the American Revolution. Eight years after helping suppress the Gordor Riots, Amherst received in 1788 what would be his last and perhaps greatest honour: he was made a baron of the United Kingdom. The township received Amherst's name in keeping with the British tradition of naming places after their heroes, although it is doubtful that Amherst ever felt a strong connection to the Chignecto region. He died on August 3, 1797 in Montreal.

EDWARD BARRON CHANDLER

Born on August 22, 1800 to parents who arrived in Nova Scotia in the Loyalist migrations, Edward Barron Chandler would go on to become one of Amherst township's best-known citizens. He went to school in Amherst, studied law, and was called to the bar in 1823. Shortly afterward, he moved to New Brunswick, where he was elected to the legislative assembly for the County of Westmorland, a seat he held from 1827 to 1836. From 1844 to 1858, he served on the executive council and gave general support to Confederation while expressing a strong dislike for the extensive powers being given to central government. He was also a New Brunswick delegate to the Charlottetown, Quebec, and London conferences on Confederation in 1864-66.

When offered a seat in the Senate in 1867, Chandler declined the opportunity, choosing instead to remain in the provincial arena. His attention soon zeroed in on the Intercolonial Railway. Like fellow Nova Scotian Joseph Howe, he longed to see a railway connecting the Maritimes with the St. Lawrence colonies, "passing wholly through British territory." Together, the two in 1851 secured an agreement to build an intercolonial railway, but the agreement was nullified by their respective governments. When guaranteed loans for the project failed to be obtained, the two provinces turned to the building of railways within their own borders.

It wasn't until 1862 that the Howe-Chandler dream was revived, and in 1864 construction of it became a condition of the Maritime Provinces' consent to enter Confederation. Work started in 1867 and, because of his interest in the project, Chandler was named commissioner in charge of construction. He saw his dream fulfilled in 1876 when the railway, however sinuous the route, was completed. Beginning at Levis, Quebec, it skirted the south shore of the St. Lawrence well away from the Maine border. At Metis, it swung down toward New Brunswick and crossed the Restigouche River at Matapedia, but not before branching east for the 85-mile dead-end run to Paspebiac on the north shore of Chaleur Bay. In New Brunswick, the line swerved through the countryside, branching at Bathurst for Caraquet and again at Derby Junction across the Miramichi. It branched again at Chatham Junction and ran straight for sixty-five miles to Moncton where it supported the older European and North American line by then running to Saint John and Shediac. The ICR then curved eastward on a fairly straight run to the Nova Scotia border and Amherst. Outside Moncton, the line swung west down the Memramcook Valley to Dorchester before looping again, intercepting Sackville, and striking across the Tantramar Marsh to Nova Scotia. This latter diversion, not unlike others over the course of the line, was said to be politically motivated, specifically by Chandler, who was then the New Brunswick member for Westmorland.

In 1878, Chandler became lieutenant governor of New Brunswick, but died before his term ended. He passed away in Fredericton on February 6, 1880.

ROBERT BARRY DICKEY

Robert Barry Dickey was born in Amherst on November 10, 1811, some eleven years after fellow townsman and Confederation colleague Edward Chandler and ten years before Charles Tupper, another fellow townsman and Confederation colleague. Educated at Windsor Academy, he began his law practice in 1834 and while he was not particularly interested in the rigours of political life, readily accepted an appointment to the legislative council, possibly at the suggestion of his good friend Tupper, who was provincial secretary. Dickey always considered the law his true calling, despite business interests in areas including lumbering, and was often called upon to give advice on questions of policy which arose in the area.

In 1864, when a Maritime union was being considered, Dickey was chosen by Tupper as the conservative delegate to the Charlottetown and, later, Quebec conferences. Documented as the most outspoken Nova Scotian critic of the Quebec plan, he believed the financial terms offered by Canada to the Maritime provinces were unjust. He continued to fight for better terms and only moved to support the Dominion when Canada offered more lucrative subsidies in 1866. As a supporter of the general principle of union, he stood behind Tupper's resolution for a final conference in London.

When the federal elections were held, Dickey opted not to seek a seat in the Commons. Instead, he accepted an appointment to the senate. Known as a wealthy man who never fully recovered after the tragic drowning of his son, he generously left the people of Amherst a parcel of land including a park and a cemetery, which remain part of his legacy in the town. He died at age 92 on July 14, 1903.

SIR CHARLES TUPPER

The original Tuppers came from England to Connecticut in 1635, but it wasn't until a century later that Sir Charles' grandfather moved to Nova Scotia to take possession of Crown lands vacated by deported Acadians. His famous grandson was born in Amherst on July 2, 1821 to Miriam Lockhart Lowe of Parrsboro and Rev. Charles Tupper, a well-known Baptist minister.

Educated at Horton Academy, Charles Tupper earned a medical degree from the University of Edinburgh in 1843 and began practicing in his native town at age 22; he was later to become the first president of the Canadian Medical Association (1867–70). In person, he was described as being "of medium height, straight, muscular and wiry, and with intense nervous energy, which gave him quickness of movement and ceaseless mental activity." A dominating personality and natural ability served him well in practice, just as physical strength and power of endurance enabled him to survive long rides on horseback through roads that were little more than narrow trails.

For twelve years, Tupper lived and worked as a general medical practitioner and soon became well-loved throughout a county which came close to worshipping him. "In my judgement," mused Wilfred Laurier in 1916, "the chief characteristic of Tupper was courage; courage which no obstacle could down, which rushed to the assault, and which, if repulsed, came back to the combat again and again; courage which never admitted defeat, and which in the midst of overwhelming disaster ever maintained the proud carriage of unconquerable defiance."

In 1855, Tupper—who was known as Cumberland Ram—decided to focus his considerable energies in the political arena and run against the able, experienced, and popular leader of the reform party, Joseph Howe. He won, but the election that brought him to the Legislative Assembly of Nova Scotia was declared void on February 24, 1857. Undaunted, the would-be politician was subsequently re-elected in a by-election that same year and was elected again in 1859 and 1863. After his victory, Tupper was given the portfolio of provincial secretary. Later, his purposeful energy carried him to the premier's seat when Johnson, the sitting premier, was made a judge in 1863.

With the head of a statesman and the heart of a philanthropist, Tupper's first public achievements were the Nova Scotia Education Acts of 1864 and 1865, which provided equitable means for the division and collection of taxes for building schools in remote districts. History gives him credit for having initiated the movement in the province toward the British North America Act; he played his part in one of the most dramatic constitutional struggles of modern times.

When the first government was being formed, Sir Charles stepped aside when it looked as though the union was about to fail. He allowed another to enter the cabinet in his place, despite the victory having been his. In the election of 1867, Sir Charles was the only conservative returned from Nova Scotia. Later, he was appointed minister of customs, followed by minister of public works in 1878, and the first minister of railways and canals in 1879.

In 1883, he was appointed high commissioner of Canada in London, a post he occupied continuously (except for one year from 1887 to 1888 as minister of finance) until 1896. Knighted in 1879, Tupper was made a baronet in 1888, and became secretary of state in the Canadian commons for three months. On May 1, 1896, he became Canada's sixth prime minister, a position he held only briefly as the government was ousted on July 8. After four years of leading the opposition, he retired. He lived in Vancouver and, later, England.

TUPPER WAS ONE OF THE FATHERS OF CONFEDERATION

In the winter of 1911-1912 while in England, he suffered an attack of bronchitis and attending doctors felt he was close to death. Yet Tupper recovered, only to receive a blow a few months later when Lady Tupper passed away. (Frances Morse Tupper was the daughter of Judge Morse, and was born at Morse's Corner.) Soon after, he paid his last visit to his hometown of Amherst when he stayed with his nephew, Charles Tupper Hillson, on Regent Street. At age 92, he was said to possess a keen interest in the news of the day, being a voracious reader of magazines and newspapers and watching with deep interest the progress of events at home and abroad.

Two years later, on October 30, 1915, the last of the fathers of Confederation died in Kent, England at age 94. The popular politician is buried in Halifax, while his mother, Marian Lockhart of Cumberland, is buried in the Amherst Cemetery. It became her final resting place in 1851. She died while Sir Charles was studying in England.

Jonathan McCully

Born in July 1809 in Maccan on land that is now occupied by a government-owned experimental farm, McCully received his early education at home and later in a grammar school in nearby Amherst which, at the time, was directed by Rev. Dr. Charles Tupper.

Although he did not attend university and was not a classical scholar, McCully possessed a fair knowledge of Latin and often quoted Latin phrases and bits of Shakespeare in his speeches and articles. In the early days when candles were scarce but provided the only source of light, it was said that McCully would sit on the hearthstone, lean against a chimney jamb, and read and study by the light of the wood fire. Like many enterprising young men of the day, he taught school as a way of further expanding his own knowledge. Interestingly, one of his earliest pupils was Charles Tupper, who would go on to join him in the ranks of the fathers of Confederation.

As a liberal, his views often conflicted with the more conservative factions that were generally more popular in the area at the time. He and James Shannon Morse—with whom he practiced law in Amherst—became well known when they waged a war of words against a pair of conservative candidates during one general election and, as a result, were harassed locally.

Eventually, McCully was appointed to the legislative council of New Brunswick where he served as solicitor general, chief commissioner for railways, and government leader in the council between 1860 and 1862. He also attended the Charlottetown, Quebec, and Westminister conferences and became a father of Confederation.

When Tupper was picking the delegates for Charlottetown, he invited Archibald, the leader of the opposition in the assembly, to name a liberal teammate. Archibald chose McCully who was, at the time, leader of the opposition in the legislative council.

After hearing the news, McCully, who was also a journalist, came back from Quebec more enthusiastic than ever for Confederation and advocated the cause in his editorials. Suddenly, the tone of the editorials was reversed; McCully was dismissed by the paper's anti-confederate proprietor, William Annand, who was then publishing Howe's "Botheration Scheme" letters as editorials. Displaced, McCully went on to serve as editor of the *Morning Journal*, renamed by him *Unionist*.

Politics continued to fascinate McCully, though, and he was called to the Canadian Senate in 1867. After a few short years, he resigned the seat in 1870 to accept an appointment as a judge of the Supreme Court of Nova Scotia, a post he retained until his death on January 2, 1877 at his home in Halifax.

ALEX COLVILLE

Internationally recognized as one of Canada's best artists and a Companion of the Order of Canada, David Alex Colville was born on August 24, 1920 in Toronto, but spent most of his youth in Amherst. The family moved there in 1929 and Colville has fond recollections of his time in the town. When *The National Post* asked several high-profile men to define their perfect woman in the February 5, 2001 edition, Colville recalled being 15 years old in Amherst and attracted to a "sweet-looking brown-haired girl, younger than I, with a dark red bicycle." He told how he confided his innocent love to his mother, and how he finally summoned the courage to present the girl with a simple gift. "My strongest memory of this short early love was of giving this girl irises picked in a swampy ditch on the eastern end of Spring Street."

Leaving the family home for post-secondary education, Colville graduated from nearby Mount Allison University in Sackville, New Brunswick, then joined the Canadian Army where he was appointed a war artist. Upon arriving in London, Colville was stationed with a supply unit in Yorkshire, subsequently travelling to the Mediterranean, Belgium, the Netherlands, and Germany. The works that stem from this time —126 of them—are housed in the art collection of the Canadian War Museum and are early examples of Colville's painstaking magic-realist style, which employs careful measurements, precise details, and cool colours.

In 1946, Colville returned to Mount Allison as an educator. He retired in 1963 but remained in the area to be close to his elderly father, who continued to live in Amherst. After his father's death in 1972, Colville and his wife, Rhoda, moved to her hometown of Wolfville. From 1981 to 1991, Colville served as a chancellor of the humanities department at Acadia University. He continues to live and paint in Wolfville.

Clarence Silliker

When Silliker, a native of Baie Verte, New Brunswick, began his building trade in the 1880s, Amherst was in the midst of growing from a small market town into an industrial centre poised to take advantage of its strategic geographic location. By 1891, the industrious craftsman was working as a builder and had entered into contract work, possibly with a partner named MacKay; the 1892 town council minutes contain several vouchers made out to Silliker and MacKay. By 1893, he had established a woodworking factory in Amherst employing fifteen to twenty men; one year later it had a workforce of 100 men. In 1904, the firm incorporated as Silliker and Company Limited.

According to *The Halifax Herald* of January 1, 1907, the company was doing well: "During the past two years, the growth of the business has been as phenomenal as the growth of the other Amherst industries. The number of men employed has increased fifty per cent, the volume of business last year aggregated a quarter of a million dollars, and the profits of the new corporation has (sic) averaged twenty per cent per year."

Although the main focus of Silliker's business was in the construction trade, he ventured into other areas as well. He opened a woodworking factory in Sackville, New Brunswick, opened a plumbing and heating department, and formed the Grand Lake Company, a large lumbering concern, with other local businessmen. Soon, Silliker was known as a leader in industrial, commercial, and public buildings, but it seems he took greatest pride in housing construction and interior fittings. His homes generally fit into three categories: modest cottages; larger, boxlike homes with hip roofs that became known as Silliker Houses; and more elaborate homes for the town's elite. Many of the latter houses line Victoria and Church streets, specifically designed and furnished with beautiful wood trim, stained glass, and fine mantelpieces.

At the peak of this construction career, Silliker's good fortune suddenly turned. Fire destroyed his factory on September 25, 1906 and while the business was valued at $70,000, it was only insured for $20,000. Although the businessman talked publicly of rebuilding, it was rumoured that he was considering leaving. Six weeks after the blaze, Silliker announced he would move to Halifax to establish a car works and by 1909, Silliker Car Works was in full operation, with Clarence serving as president, and his son Elmore as secretary-treasurer. The product line included railway cars, machine work and castings, marine repairs, and wood items. Although Silliker was once estimated to have the largest payroll in Halifax, historian R.D. Tennant notes the the company was "in real trouble" four years after its incorporation. In 1901, Silliker turned the business over to J.R. Douglas of Amherst, who reorganized it as the Nova Scotia Car Works Limited. It failed by 1922. Silliker then returned to Amherst, where his final years were spent selling truckloads of building supplies ranging from British Columbia cedar doors to car parts, machinery, and furniture. He died in 1927 with little notice, but his legacy lives on in Amherst architecture.

RAIL TRANSPORTATION

The passage of the Intercolonial Railway through the district in 1872 began a period of industrial expansion and entrepreneurial optimism in Amherst that has not yet been exceeded. Within forty years, Amherst went from being a small, largely self-sufficient community, to the most progressive industrialized town in eastern Canada. It quickly earned itself the well-deserved sobriquet "Busy Amherst."

A great deal of this expansion was based on the proximity of the railway, and many of the major industries were established along the right of way. In fact, tracing the route of the present CNR, which mirrors the route of the ICR, shows that a purposeful effort was made to bring the railway through the centre of town.

Swinging around the foot of the Aulac Ridge, the railway runs straight across the Missaquash Marsh. Rather than skirt the foot of the Fort Lawrence Ridge, the line cuts through it and emerges at the Amherst Marsh. A serpentine S curve then swings it eastward, where it enters the town on the final curve of the S by cutting across the Post Road as it climbs the grade into Amherst. The acute angle between the railway embankment and the Post Road (LaPlanche Street) precluded the building of a crossing to maintain the integrity of the road. Instead, Lower LaPlanche Street was swung westward to cross the railway at right angles at Foundry Street. Then, 400 yards of new road were constructed to connect with the Post Road where it emerged from under the west side of the railway embankment. Finally, after crossing the LaPlanche River downstream from the new trestle, the road continued parallel to the railway for another mile before crossing to the east side of the railway again at what became known as the second crossing. It wasn't until the summer of 1932 that the "New Road" (now old Highway #2), was opened between Lower LaPlanche Street and the second crossing on the east side of the railway, and the old Sackville Road was subsequently abandoned as the main arterial route to the province.

THE INTERCOLONIAL RAILWAY STATION IN AMHERST

Trains travelling this route would stop at the town's first station, located a short distance south from the site of the current station on Station Street. It was constructed of local sandstone from a quarry on upper Church Street. (The Donalds' quarry, which became the major supplier of the local stone, did not open for another five years, in 1891.)

When Canadian National Railway took over the line, Amherst Sandstone Quarry and T.D. and D.R. Leblanc were awarded the contract to build a two-storey depot which included separate waiting rooms for men and women.

THE ROYAL VISIT, 1939 Amherstonians arrived at the train station en masse to attend the royal visit of King George V and Queen Elizabeth to Nova Scotia. Here, the couple waves to the crowd during that 1939 trip aboard the royal train.

Nelson A. Rhodes

Born in Amherst, Nelson A. Rhodes was the son of John and Parmelia (Parker) Rhodes. He began his education in the town, but after the death of his parents, the 13-year-old went to live with his sister in Sackville, New Brunswick, to continue his early schooling. He later returned to Amherst to learn a carpenter's trade. At the age of 20, Rhodes went to Boston, where he followed the trade as a journeyman and superintendent for ten years. Records show he was also employed as an architect during that period.

In 1872, he married Sarah Davison Curry, the sister of his future business partner, Nathanial Curry. The couple had three children, two of whom died before 1900. In 1877, the time came to return home to Amherst and it was here Rhodes began a business as a carpenter and builder. By 1893, a partnership with his brother-in-law was incorporated as Rhodes, Curry Company, which would go on to become one of the largest and most important businesses in the province, employing nearly six hundred people.

An initial director of Canada Electric Company Limited along with D.W. Robb, the community-minded Rhodes was a member of the Masonic order, belonging to the Amherst lodge, and also to the I.O.O.F., where he filled all the chairs. He also served as mayor of the town in 1904, and for many years served on the board of governors of Acadia University. He donated a building, known as Rhodes Hall, to the university, which itself features many buildings constructed by Rhodes, Curry Company.

Rhodes passed away on Sept. 30, 1909 at the age of 64. His death was caused by what is now known as appendicitis. Had he been properly treated, he would have likely lived many more years. A doctor was dispatched by special train from Montreal to tend to Rhodes, but he arrived too late to be of assistance.

Highland View Hospital

The history of Amherst's first hospital is a colourful, albeit short, one. Construction of the building began in 1903, was completed in 1904 at a cost of $20,000 and operated for just 24 years before fire destroyed it in 1928. Steps were immediately taken to replace it and a new hospital—presented to the town by Senator R.B. Dickey—was opened on the same site just one year later. The name was suggested by its location on high ground, removed from the downtown core. In the beginning, the hospital had two public wards for adults, a children's ward, and eleven private wards. The total capacity was thirty patients. Ten doctors (Avard, Bliss, Dyas, Hewson, MacDougall, MacKinnon, MacQueen, Mitchell, Miller, and Morse) ran the facility with the help of five nurses and an annual maintenance bill of $8,000. The operating room was furnished by the Ladies' Hospital Aid Society at a cost of $1,600. Area residents are now eagerly awaiting the end of construction to yet another new hospital. Located in Upper Nappan, the state-of-the-art care facility is expected to open soon.

D.W. Robb A well-respected man in the town, D.W. Robb (the son of Alexander Robb, founder of A. Robb Foundry and later Robb Engineering) was active in many aspects of life in Amherst. The town's first fire chief, he held the position until the late 1890s when he resigned and accepted a position in the United States. He was succeeded at the fire department by Alex Bonnyman.

This was during the same period that he served as president and chief engineer in the company founded by his father. He was named to the posts in 1890. Aside from his duties with the fire department and at the company, an article in the June 29, 1903 edition of an Amherst newspaper tells of how he helped change at least one mode of transportation in the town: "About 20 years ago (1883), D.W. Robb introduced the high-wheel bicycle of the skyscraper class in town. For some weeks, they were followed all around town by a number of people, especially small boys who would gaze with awe on them as the riders went round the streets. A few years later, if we mistake not, introduced the safety bicycle in our town."

SENATOR HANCE LOGAN

The senator, known to some admirers as Handsome Hance, was born April 26, 1869 at the Logan homestead in Amherst Point, the son of James Archibald Logan and Hannah Hunter. Educated at Model School in Truro, Pictou Academy, and Dalhousie University, he was called to the bar in 1892 and appointed King's counsel in 1909. Described as tall, aggressive, and colourful, Logan was said to be something of an athlete in his younger days, although he was not a strong man and tired frequently with age.

Logan's law career began in Amherst, where he was a director with a number of industrial concerns. He consulted with no less than Thomas A. Edison in Orange, New Jersey in regard to the theory of transporting power by wire over the bankhead of a coal mine. Records of the day show that at least partial credit is due to Logan for being able to persuade the co-directors of Maritime Coal, Railway & Power Company to build a power plant at the Chignecto coal mine to produce electricity for industries in Amherst and other areas. Later, he received a telegram of congratulations from Edison on the inauguration of the first power plant on the American continent for the generation of electricity at the mouth of a coal mine, and the distribution of that power to other centres.

In his political life, Logan was an avowed Liberal and in 1896, at age 27, became the first Liberal elected to the House of Commons from Cumberland County, a territory long held by Sir Charles Tupper. This was the start of thirty years of public service. Re-elected in 1900, 1904, and 1908, he lost in 1911 on the reciprocity issue, but won again in 1921 with a 5,355 majority, at the time the largest ever taken in the province in a general election. This was seen as something of a great comeback for Logan.

An avid traveller, the politician was present by invitation at the coronation in Westminster Abbey of King Edward and Queen Alexandra in 1902. He was later presented to King George V. At ease as a public speaker, Logan was appointed to the Senate in 1929 where the simple language he used was said to appeal to the ordinary person.

RHODES, CURRY FIRE DEPARTMENT

Vast resources allowed the Rhodes, Curry Company to finance its own fire department—a valuable contribution to the townspeople in the days when fires were all too common and could devastate businesses and wipe out fortunes. Here, 26 early firefighters pose outside the No. 3 Fire Station.

EMIL WOLF

In 1883, J. Emil (Amy) Wolf began a long career at Robb Engineering that would help secure him a place in *Ripley's Believe It or Not*. Born in Germany in 1860, he started apprenticing to be a blacksmith in 1874 with the German State Railway and went on to run Robb's forge shop for more than sixty years. In 1949, Ripley's recognized Wolf for having been a blacksmith for 75 years.

Chapter 5

Amherst Schools

St. Charles School

The St. Charles School on Prince Arthur Street holds happy memories for many who were educated within its stone walls. Opened in 1906, it was soon found to be too small, so by May 1914, an extension and other renovations were started. They included the removal of a tower roof as well as an addition on the west side that mirrored the east side. Modification to the main roof allowed the construction of an auditorium and stage, which was altered at a later time to accommodate the commercial studies classroom. The brick chimney was removed from the main roof and a lantern-style bell tower was constructed, with the bell pull-rod extending through a pipe to a handle on the first floor at the south corner of the hallway jog. These renovations provided modern classroom space for grades one to eight, with commercial studies located on the top floor. The classrooms were large and airy, with high, transomed windows that could be opened at the bottom, allowing plenty of air and light to circulate as studies were undertaken.

AMHERST ACADEMY

Amherst Academy came into being after being approved at a ratepayers' meeting in the YMCA Hall on November 5, 1891, when records show that teachers' salaries hovered around $275 annually. By comparison, principals earned the princely sum of nearly $1,000. Rhodes, Curry Company was selected as the builder of the academy, with the cornerstone laid by the Masonic Lodge in 1892. The building opened in 1893 and the result was impressive. The three-storey structure measured 128 feet long and 71 feet deep, topped by a cupola in which hung a bell reputed to have come from a two-storey church in Fort Beausejour. With its 11-foot ceilings, the basement contained a laboratory, playrooms, sanitary closets, a janitor's room, coal bins, and six large furnaces for heating the building. Six high school classrooms, a library, and office were situated on the first floor. The second floor was set aside for six elementary classrooms, and the third, for an assembly hall with stage and dressing rooms. In keeping with the order of the day, the new building offered separation of the sexes in all hallways, as well as on staircases and playground.

AMHERST ACADEMY TEACHERS AND STAFF, LATE 1890S

CHILDREN DOING GYMNASTICS ON THE ACADEMY GROUNDS IN THE 1940S

**Ratchford Private Boarding School for Young Ladies—
Amherst Female Seminary**

Education began on a humble scale in Amherst. For those intent on having their children become acquainted with the three Rs, small private schools for boys were among the only earliest forms of formal education offered in the town. Parents were charged with the task of finding innovative ways of paying the teachers. Often, this was done by boarding them for a set time, buying a few supplies or even making a small payment of money.

By the early 1850s, education for young women began to take a more formal shape under the capable tutelage of Mrs. Caroline E. Ratchford and her sister, Miss Yates. Another pair of sisters, Mrs. Dr. Carritte and Mrs. Stubbs, also taught.

Sitting on the site at the corner of Victoria and Acadia streets (the present-day National Specialty property), the Amherst Female Seminary boarded about thirty girls, with most specializing in French, English, and music. Other subjects included astronomy, classic literature, and needlework.

In a review of education in the 1850s published in the October 31, 1973 issue of *The Citizen*, a local newspaper, Dr. G.P. Hennessey pointed to an old advertisement: "Mrs. C.E. Ratchford begs to notice that she intends opening a female seminary after the Christmas vacation in the village of Amherst for the instruction of young ladies in the ordinary and higher branches of education ... Amherst is a remarkably healthy part of the province and in that respect, possesses advantages over a town residence, especially for children of a delicate constitution." Indeed, the seminary served a vital role since public schools would not come into existence until after the Free School Act passed as a party measure by Sir Charles Tupper in 1864.

Acadia Street Academy

The original high school stood on the grounds of Acadia Street School until 1892. When it was torn down in 1904, the front section of Acadia Street School was built, with the back portion being added in 1914.

Duke Street School

A building of four departments was erected on Duke Street in 1903, with two rooms completed and occupied that year and the remaining two in 1904.

EARLY EDUCATORS — EDWARD JAMES LAY WITH MISS LIZZIE SKIMMINGS, MISS COVE, MISS ADA TRAVIS, MISS BELL AND MISS CRANE.

EARLY EDUCATION

Educators were revered in the late 1800s and early 1900s. From all accounts, Edward James Lay, one of the leading educators of the province, was among the most eminent and beloved. He is shown here in this photo with (in random order) Miss Lizzie Skimmings, Miss Cove (Mrs. Bonnyman); Miss Ada Travis; Miss Bell (Mrs. C. McLeod) and Miss Crane (Mrs. R.R. Tremane).

Lay, a self-taught teacher, began his career in education at age 16 when he became a teacher in Jeddore, Halifax County. Early on, he took a year off to attend King's College, later passing examinations for a bachelor of arts degree; he never obtained the coveted letters, though, since he was unable to afford to spend another year at university.

After having charge of several small country schools, he became principal of Annapolis Academy in 1879 and principal of Cumberland County Academy in 1881. He resigned in 1886 to become inspector of schools in Cumberland and Colchester, often walking twenty miles a day while visiting schools. In 1892, he returned to Amherst again to become principal of Cumberland County Academy and was appointed as Supervisor of Schools for the town in 1912, a position he held until his sudden death on October 19, 1919.

While he rose to administrative posts, Lay was, first and foremost, an educator. For years, it was said that not a weeknight went by where a student was not found in his book-lined study receiving extra help to make the grade in college. Due to his efforts, a flourishing public library—The Lay Library—was started. He was also responsible for compiling a house-to-house census so that every child of school age would be educated.

WEST HIGHLANDS SCHOOL

Built in 1912 to accommodate the rapid expansion of the West Highlands area of town, and to fulfill an election promise of then mayor Thomas Lowther, this school was originally constructed as a junior high. While under construction, classes were held in the Duke Street School and, for a short time, in an abandoned suspender factory. The relocation and ensuing wait were said to be worthwhile. Designed by architect Leslie R. Fairn of Aylesford, Nova Scotia and constructed by contractor Victor Wood Works Company, the new school created from Pugwash brick, reinforced concrete, and a metal roof measured 89 feet by 148 feet. Rather than showcasing old-fashioned features such as cloakrooms, the building was the height of modernity with broad corridors, vented wardrobes, and self-balanced rolling fronts providing storage for students' clothing in the thirteen classrooms. Each classroom door was also equipped with a peephole so that the principal and others might look in on the room without disturbing the studies.

Chapter 6

Historic Churches

HIGHLAND BAPTIST CHURCH

Highland Baptist Church has a long tradition in the Town of Amherst. First known as a mission, this part of the Baptist church was active with a large Sunday School, missionary society, youth group, men's brotherhood, and sewing circle, all of which connected the parish community and forged strong ties among parishioners. Records of the Sunday School show industrious members were able to finance the group by buying supplies, which also helped pay for part of the fuel bill. One particular class of girls, under the capable guidance of Miss Agatha Peacock, gave more than $100 on several occasions to missions.

FIRST BAPTIST CHURCH

The parishes founded in Amherst in the 1700s were said to be primarily of two faiths: Presbyterian and Baptist. A church that stands as a landmark in downtown Amherst was built in 1895 by Rhodes, Curry Company to the specifications of a design by Harry Mott of Saint John. The dimensions of the Queen Anne Revival style First Baptist Church are 122 feet by 70 feet, and the details are many: turreted towers reaching 75 and 100 feet, spacious portals gracing a semi-circular balcony, wonderfully-proportioned gables, and spectacular stained glass. The much-anticipated service of dedication was conducted by Dr. D.A. Steele, a longtime pastor of the church, on September 1 of that year, attracting 1,500 people. Notably, the first regular minister of the earlier church was Rev. Charles Tupper, father of Sir Charles Tupper. By 1896, the congregation stood at 537.

The church, while magnificent, was not the first for area Baptists. The land on which the church stands at 66 Victoria Street was donated by Philip Freeman in 1809 to any religious group who needed it and, after a decade, White Hall emerged. It took some $2,000 in labour and supplies to construct the box-like, 42-foot-square structure with a double row of windows.

A more traditional-style church took its place in 1863. Built for $8,000, it was known for the 140-foot spire that dominated the skyline. By 1875, the spire was removed when it was discovered that its excessive flexibility in the wind was rending the entire front of the church. Measuring 80 feet by 45 feet, the building seated 600 people, but the congregation soon proved too large for the dimensions. The building was moved behind the present Baptist church and renovated by B.C. Munroe into a theatre which came to be known as the Academy of Music and featured vaudeville acts.

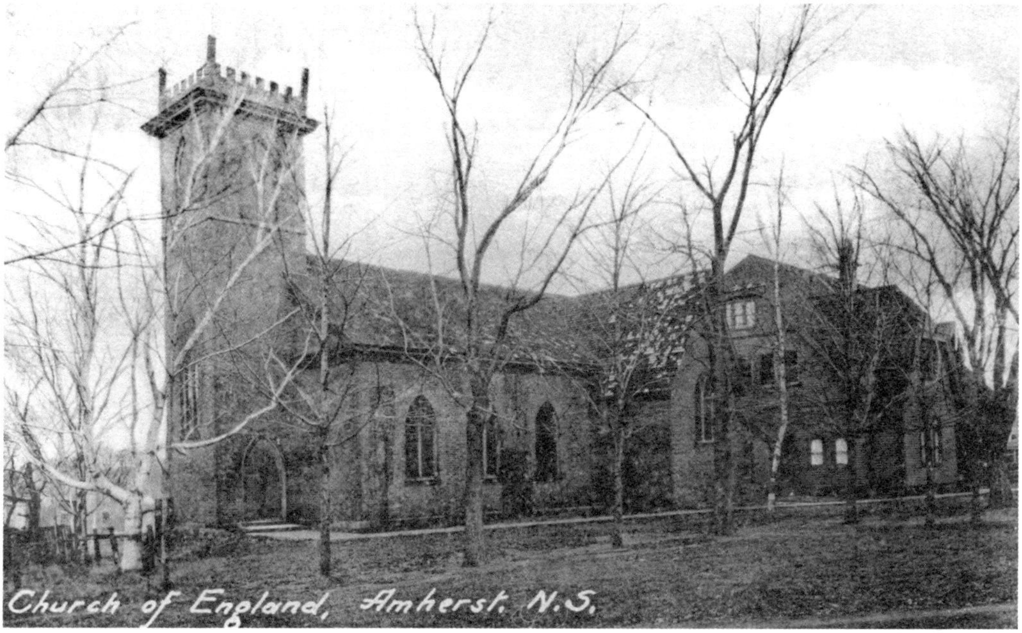

Church of England

In 1750, the Society for the Propagation of the Gospel sent an Anglican priest to Fort Lawrence and the Amherst area. The first recorded visit dates back to June 1752 when Rev. Thomas Wood held a service in the Chignecto area and was welcomed by four hundred people who celebrated the baptisms of 27 children.

By 1822, Rev. John Burnyeat and the Honourable James Morse were instrumental in having the first church built in West Amherst. Constructed by George Revelle, an Englishman who was then building several brick houses in the vicinity, it was located next to the Anglican burying ground on property purchased in 1826 from Charles Baker.

As the structure aged, Rev. George Townshend, a longtime minister to the church, attempted to have it replaced by a new building. In the end, though, it was decided to merely dismantle the edifice in 1846. The bricks were carted to Victoria Square to a one-eighth-acre parcel of land donated by Kniffen Purdy. There, the church was reconstructed in time to celebrate its first service on Christmas Day, 1846.

It wasn't until 31 years later that a new chancel was constructed, designed by P.W. St. George, son-in-law of Canon Townshend and also engineer for the City of Montreal. Today, the church, located at 60 Victoria Street, remains important architecturally for its style, a vernacular interpretation of the crucifix floor plan employing two styles of brick bond.

ST. CHARLES ROMAN CATHOLIC CHURCH

St. Charles Roman Catholic church

The history of the Roman Catholic faith in Amherst is traced back as far as 1848 when Rev. Townshend wrote in his journal of July 30 that "the Romish service [was] performed here by the Roman bishop for the first time as far as I know in this village."

By 1878, the area had its first priest in Father Donnelly (who remains known for building the rectory beside the church), although it wasn't until 1889 that the cornerstone for St. Charles Roman Catholic Church was laid on land donated by Dr. James Paige, a recent convert to Catholicism. It is said that the good doctor gave the land after most others refused to sell to the church. However, the move eventually caused so much bitterness and made Dr. Paige so unpopular that, in 1849, he gave up his local practice and moved with his family to Halifax.

In 1892, the building featuring the first stone from the Donalds' quarry east of Willow Street in its basement was finally completed. On April 30, 1893, the church was named for Saint Charles Borromeo, and Cornelius O'Brien, Archbishop of Halifax, opened the ceremonies. A school operated by the Sisters of Charity was later placed behind the church, a glebe house was erected to the north of the church, and a stone wall surrounded the complex.

Trinity Methodist Church

By 1876, the wooden structure of Trinity Methodist Church was built to serve a growing congregation in the town. The official opening of the doors was greatly welcomed by Methodists who had first met in the original Baptist church in 1819, and then on the Douglas property on Victoria Street in 1841. According to the Chignecto Post of 1878, the old Methodist church was moved from Victoria to "the site of the Mason Hall, which was recently burned and will be used as a public hall."

The cornerstone for Trinity Methodist Church (shown below) was laid in 1906 and the edifice was officially opened for religious services on September 22, 1907, replacing the earlier wooden version built in 1876. Designed by architect C.B. Chappell and constructed by James Reid of Sydney, who erected it using red sandstone facing and trim, the building sets forth the Gothic Revival style which had been imported from Britain and flourished in Canada for many years. Elements of this design include the pointed, arch crowned windows and doorways (also reflected in the castellated turret with contrasting stonework). Interestingly, it incorporates a pair of windows from the Methodist church on the south facade and a pair of lower rectangular windows from the Presbyterian church on the north facade.

During the construction period, workers' activity was under the daily scrutiny of neighbours, who were anxious after the Havelock Street facade apparently fell onto the street with a noise that frightened them into assuming the rumble stemmed from an earthquake!

Once complete, the Methodist church served its own congregation for many years. A United church union took place in 1925, although the Presbyterian and Methodist congregations met separately until 1936. By 1957, the Fort Lawrence United Church had also joined the congregation. Two other groups—Grace Methodist and St. Paul's Presbyterian—joined in West Highlands to form Immanuel United Church.

Chapter 7

Special Events

MARCHING OFF

Lusby Street was part of the route taken by World War One soldiers marching off to the Amherst train station, where transportation awaited them en route to war and an experience that would change their lives forever.

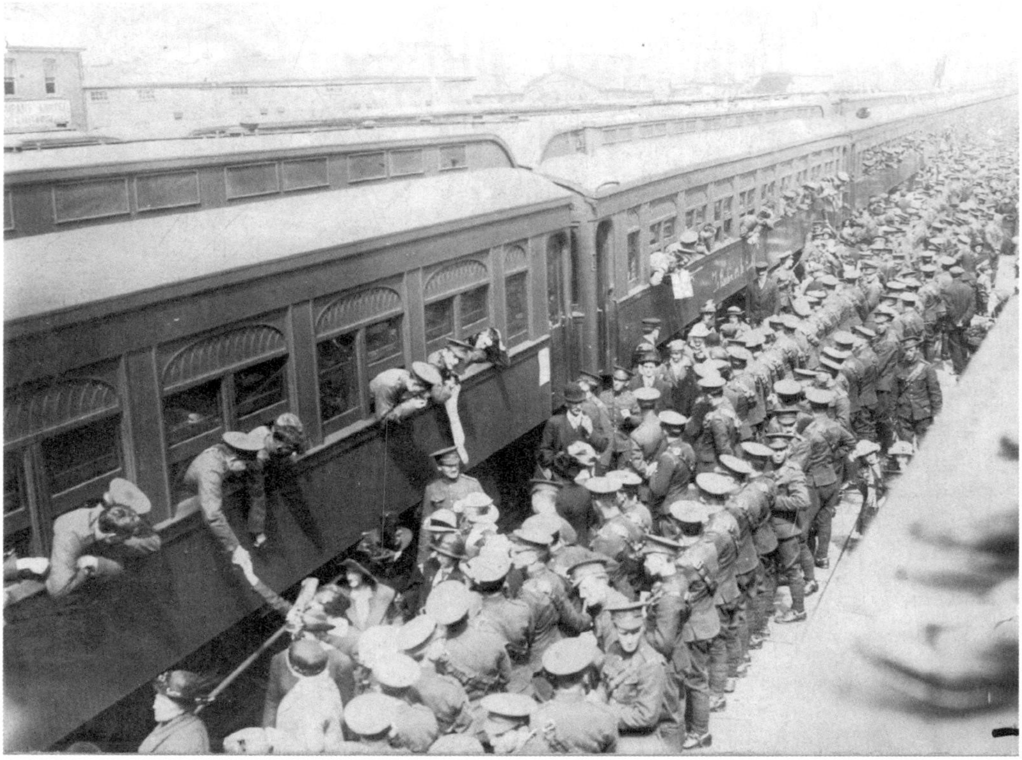

The Long Goodbye

World War One soldiers are seen departing the Amherst railway station as those who would be left behind say goodbye, perhaps for the final time. Known as "The War to End All Wars," it would rage on for four years, leaving in its wake a toll of death and destruction such as the world had never seen. Amherst was a basic training centre in World War One. Situated on the main railway line, it was adjacent to the marshes, with their intervening ridges offering a natural terrain for military manoeuvres. The town also contributed to the war effort in other ways. Local recruits were eventually posted to the 106th Batallion Nova Scotia Rifles, the 85th Nova Scotia Highland Batallion, or the 25th Batallion. The presence of the 22nd Batallion (Van-Doo) in Amherst from February 1915 until they sailed for the United Kingdom later that year was an interim arrangement to remove them from Valcartier Camp in Quebec.

Amherst
Armouries

Dancing

February 5th.
1917.

AMHERST ARMOURY

Like many of its kind built throughout the Dominion around 1904-1905, the armoury was built on land donated by the town. Aside from its military use, it also played host to black-tie balls and gala events. This pocket-sized dance card from February 5, 1917 shows that chaperones Mrs. Foster, Mrs. Tennant and Mrs. McLeod were in attendance. Mrs. Foster's husband was Captain Archie Foster, in France at the time of the dance; he returned from the war and was eventually appointed postmaster in Amherst. The program included a grand march, and dances as varied as the one-step, a tag two-step, and various waltzes. Men who were successful in being granted a dance by the holder of a dance card would have their name written in pencil beside the promised dance.

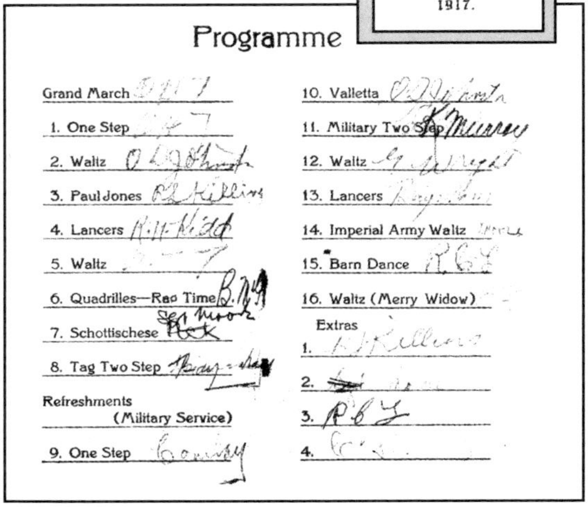
Programme

Grand March
1. One Step
2. Waltz
3. Paul Jones
4. Lancers
5. Waltz
6. Quadrilles—Rag Time
7. Schottischese
8. Tag Two Step
Refreshments
(Military Service)
9. One Step
10. Valletta
11. Military Two Step
12. Waltz
13. Lancers
14. Imperial Army Waltz
15. Barn Dance
16. Waltz (Merry Widow)
Extras
1.
2.
3.
4.

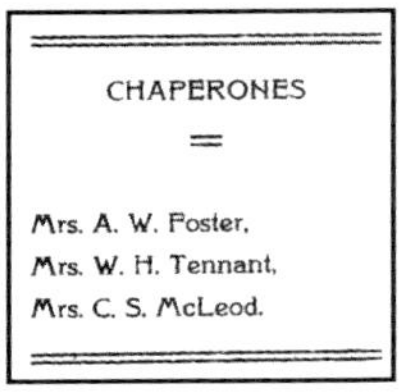
CHAPERONES

Mrs. A. W. Foster,
Mrs. W. H. Tennant,
Mrs. C. S. McLeod.

INTERNMENT CAMP

One of Canada's largest prisoner of war camps was located at the then-defunct Malleable Iron Foundry, which lay between the railway and Park Street. Part of the original building is still used by Casey Concrete, and much of the present-day Casey storage yard was part of the fenced P.O.W compound. The facility, which opened April 17, 1915 and closed September 27, 1919, was quickly converted to house more than eight hundred men during World War One. Prisoners appear to have been well-fed and photographs such as this one show that they organized recreational clubs and hosted revues where they dressed in costume.

FENCING CLUB

The prisoners kept fit through participating in various sporting activities, one of which was organized as a camp fencing club. Here, the prisoners of war are clad in the appropriate dress and preparing to begin.

Officers of the Internment Camp

The internment camp consisted of a building that was one hundred feet wide by a quarter mile long. These officers would have been housed in the south end officers' quarters, close to the camp hospital and the medical inspection room. The north end housed the prisoners quarters and their washrooms. Further to the north, close to Patterson Street, was the large mess hall, recreation room, kitchen, and pantry stores.

Back row, l-r: Lieut. Harold Major; Lieut. Burton Elliott Goodwin, medical officer; Captain M.B. Anderson; and Lieut. Charles Wesley Kierstead.

Front row, l-r: Lieut. Jennings; Captain H.H. Hawkins or Hopkins; Colonel Commandant A.D. Morris; Captain Frederick Carman Wightman, adjutant; and unknown.

RIOT AT THE CAMP

An undercurrent of dissent in the internment camp was evident despite the joviality. In June 1915, a riot broke out during which one person was killed and four others were wounded. An inquiry held after the incident found that discipline was poor and likely to blame for the tragedy. As a result, the camp commandant was relieved of command and in 1916, the prisoners were put to work clearing land at the Nappan Experimental Farm, helping improve Dickey Park, and working for Canadian National Rail Company. Their contribution to the farm is clearly indicated in the following passage from a 1917 annual report:
"The greater portion of the land clearing during the past season was done by prisoners of war, who are interned in Amherst. They are brought out to the farm by train in the morning and taken back at night under escort. Owing to their labour being voluntary, the number varies from 75 to 200 per day. They worked from August 25 to December 16, as the weather permitted." In the end, 16 acres of heavily stumped land was cleared, piled, and burned. Five acres were chopped down out of green forest, part of which had been burned through with forest fire. Another 30 acres of rough land was levelled with pick and shovel.

Leon Trotsky

One of the most famous war prisoners held in Amherst was Leon Trotsky (shown in this photograph, fourth from the left in the back row), who would go on to aid Nikolai Lenin to victory during the Russian Revolution. He was held in the Amherst camp for about a month in 1917. The following passage comes from his autobiography, *My Life*: "The Amherst concentration camp was located in an old and very dilapidated iron foundry that had been confiscated from its German owner. The sleeping bunks were arranged in three tiers, two deep, on each side of the hall. About eight hundred of us lived in these conditions. The air in this improvised dormitory at night can be imagined. Men hopelessly clogged the passages, elbowing their way through, lay down or got up, played cards or chess. Many of them practised crafts, some with extraordinary skill. I still have, stored in Moscow, some things made by Amherst prisoners. And yet, in spite of the heroic efforts of the prisoners to keep themselves physically and morally fit, five of them had gone insane. We had to eat and sleep in the same room with these madmen."

The Chignecto Ship Railway Story

CHIGNECTO SHIP RAILWAY

The Fort Lawrence dock site was a busy place on September 11, 1890. The water in the lower left of the photograph is part of the broader holding basin excavation, and would have little effect on the work in the lifting dock pit (centre) at the far end. The steam shovel in the middle foreground is in the process of filling tip cars serried along the rail line, while some men to the right appear to be laying or removing another section of track. Smoke from several steam winch boilers rises above the horizon, and the engine and boiler house, with its 80-foot brick smokestack, towers above the landscape. The dimensions of the combined dock and holding basin excavations were about 775 feet long by a maximum of 350 feet wide and from 40 to 60 feet deep.

HENRY KETCHUM

Fredericton engineer Henry George Clopper Ketchum had a dream. As he visualized it, an innovative ship railway would carry vessels up to two thousand tons overland across the Isthmus of Chignecto, saving seven hundred miles on a Montreal to Saint John trip and three hundred miles on a similar journey to Boston or Portland. The project was nearly complete when, in 1891, financial problems brought about its demise.

That realization was a bitter one for Ketchum. His final plan called for a railway 17 miles long, with a dock, a ship-holding basin, and lifting machinery at each end. The Fort Lawrence basin was 530 feet long, 300 feet wide, and was excavated to a depth of

40 feet. Two gates 30 feet high would span a 60-foot gap at the outer end of this basin to maintain a working level of water in the dock. At Tidnish, the basin would be dredged offshore. The lifting docks would be situated at the inner end of the basins. Niches let into the masonry of the identical docks would house the 20 lifting rams from which a massive steel grid would be suspended. The grid contained the rails on which would sit the cradle transporter. The entire apparatus would be sunk to the bed of the dock and a ship floated over it. When the grid and cradle were raised under the ship, keel and bilge blocks would support the hull and the grid would be raised to track level, where hydraulically operated iron chocks would be shot under the ends of the grid beams to lock it to the masonry.

The cradles could be assembled up to three sections, depending upon the size of the ship to be transported. The raised ship and cradle would be drawn off the grid by hydraulic capstans, and two locomotives would be coupled to the front of the cradle to begin a ten-mile-per-hour trip across the isthmus.

Ketchum was a man with a dream that eventually died due to financial difficulties, but he continued to be optimistic about its possibilities should funding ever come through: "All fears of the practicality of the ship railway and injury to vessel will disappear as if by magic with the transport of the first loaded vessel from gulf to bay."

SHIP RAILROAD DOCK NEAR AMHERST

KETCHUM SOLVES FLOATING BOG PROBLEM

This half-mile stretch of floating bog in the Long Lake/Round Lake district, some six miles east of the Fort Lawrence dock, presented a formidable obstacle in that it required the removal of the floating mat of vegetation. Filling the bog over the mat would have carried it to the bottom under the weight of the fill, where it would have eventually rotted and jeopardized the integrity of the embankment.

Bedrock was located from eight to twenty feet down and was covered by a thick, gas-generating layer of plant detritus that was too fine and soluble to dredge. In order to ensure a good bond between bedrock and the rock and earth fill, a section of the bog was filled and brought up to grade level. Then an excavation was made down through the embankment to bedrock, where it was found that the detritus had been displaced and the bond was sound.

The above photo, taken on September 20, 1890, shows the fill tips advancing from the east. The bright line just below the woods on the left is the Round Lake run coming down to cross the right of way and empty into Long Lake. A water control structure was inserted under the embankment to carry the excess water out of the bog.

Building the culvert on the Tidnish River

The erection of the Tidnish River culvert between the limbs of the river's loops can be appreciated when viewing the solid earth at the end of the masonry. A pit was excavated inside the loop to facilitate the laying of sill stones and the lower courses of the spandrel walls. This site was isolated from the river current and the rise and fall of the tide.

Since some seepage could be anticipated through the sandy sub-strata, a steam pump was set up to drain the excavation during erection of the lower courses of the masonry. The iron pipe connected to the pump (out of the photo) can be seen, near right.

The two men are standing on the bevelled surface of the first course of the arch. Before erection of the arch could proceed very far beyond this point the wooden centring must be inserted to support successive courses of the arch, prior to them being locked in by the keystones.

Erecting the Arch over the Culvert

A number of water control structures were required along the right of way, the largest of these being the 30-foot spandrel arch masonry culvert erected to span the Tidnish River. This culvert was located inside a long loop of the river on relatively dry ground. Once completed, it was only necessary to divert the course of the river through the arch, fill in the old bed, and raise the embankment across the flood plain.

Taken on October 24, 1890, the photograph above shows the process of erecting the arch by supporting the arch stones on wooden centring until the keystone for each course was inserted and the arch became self-supporting. The lines of masonry buttresses, seen at left, were in place to reduce uneven stress in the arch when it came under load. These would be hidden in the rubble backfill when the culvert was completed and the roadbed was raised above it.

THE GREAT AMHERST MYSTERY

Every small town has its tale to tell, but few local legends are able to terrify as much as the story of Esther Cox, a young woman who would go on to draw international attention as the victim of a bizarre twist of fate. This classic account of possession and exorcism is chilling for one reason: the strange events actually occurred and were documented by thousands of people.

It all began in 1878 when Esther was a happy 18-year-old living with her sister and brother-in-law, Olive and Daniel Teed, their children, and another sister, Jennie. A fun-loving girl, Esther enjoyed playing with her nephews and visiting friends. Like many other girls of the time, she busied herself with household chores at the Princess Street home and attended church regularly. The tranquility and simplicity of this ordinary life was shattered when an unexplainable phenomena made her the target of its cruelty.

THE PRINCESS STREET HOME OF ESTHER COX

Esther began to be haunted by unseen spirits. They engraved death threats into her bedroom wall, swelled her limbs in feverish fits, stuck her with pins, chased her with kitchen knives, set fires in the house, and pounded on the roof with a sound so thunderous it would awaken neighbours and attract crowds of curious people. Initially, Esther sought refuge with friends and family, but the demons soon followed her. In 1879, a neighbour's barn that Esther had been working in caught fire and was destroyed. Charged with arson, she was convicted and spent a month in jail.

Many attested to her innocence since it had become obvious that an unearthly force was diligently at work. Entire congregations witnessed flying hymn books in church on the Sundays Esther attended; locals and outsiders alike saw demons perform at White's Oyster Saloon on LaPlanche Street where Esther worked—chairs would become animated and stack themselves in front of amazed patrons while dishes would dance and then smash on the floor.

Esther and her mysterious manifestations drew international curiosity and it became fashionable for people to visit the town and witness these strange and incredible events firsthand. The tale evoked skepticism and Esther was labelled a fraud, a lunatic, a criminal, and even a conductor of lightning as society struggled to find an explanation for what was happening to her.

Amazingly enough, Esther survived the demonization and went on to become a wife and mother who finally took up residence in the United States. Still, The Great Amherst Mystery remains unsolved, locked beyond our narrow understanding of our world and the spirit world.

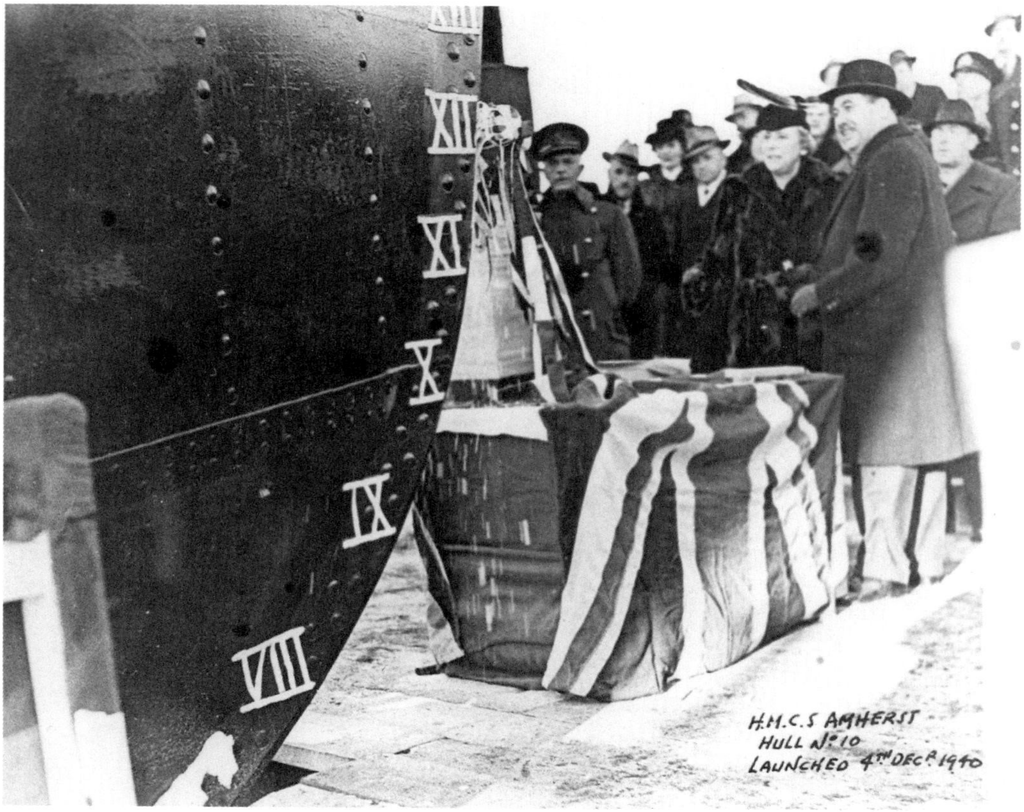

H.M.C.S. ***Amherst***

The H.M.C.S. *Amherst* was launched December 4, 1940. Following commissioning in August 1941, the destroyer arrived at Halifax on August 22 and after working up, joined Newfoundland Command in October. *Amherst* was steadily employed as an ocean escort for the next three years, and was involved in two particularly hard-fought convoy battles. In August 1942, *Amherst* joined EG C-4. The only real respite came between May and November 1943 when the ship underwent a major refit at Charlottetown, including the extension of the fo'c'sle. After workups at Pictou, *Amherst* returned to the North Atlantic until September 1944, when it began another long refit in Liverpool, Nova Scotia. Following workups in Bermuda in January 1945, the ship joined Halifax Force, but was lent to EG C-7 in March for one round trip to the United Kingdom. It was paid off July 16, 1945 at Sydney, and placed in reserve at Sorel. After being sold in 1946, the ship served the Venezuelan Navy until it was broken up in 1956. In all, H.M.C.S. *Amherst* spent 703 days at sea with the Royal Canadian Navy and travelled 140,000 nautical miles.

Chapter 8

Sports, Leisure, and Entertainment

CORONATION DAY PARADE, AUGUST 9, 1902

Formed in 1883, the Amherst Fire Department is one of the oldest in the Atlantic Provinces, with the original department including volunteers from Citizens' Band and Robb's Foundry. Throughout its history, the department has been actively involved in the community history as well as in firefighters' sports with people from all walks of life serving within its ranks. One of the town's most respected businessmen, D.W. Robb, assumed the post of the department's first chief (a post he held for years) with Fred Carter as the first secretary. The department operated out of the No. 1 Fire Station on Church Street, which was used as the headquarters, complemented by the No. 2 Fire Station (remembered as the location of an emergency horse-drawn pumper on LaPlanche Street) and the No. 3 Fire Station at the corner of Albion and Pleasant streets.

NELLIE SARGEANT AND HER ELDEST DAUGHTER, VIVIAN, ON CHRISTIE'S POND IN AUGUST 1908

CHRISTIE'S POND

Fed by warm springs and an accompanying brook, the picturesque and well-loved Christie's Pond served a utilitarian purpose in the town since it provided power for a waterwheel used by the Christie brothers to operate machinery in the mill and woodworking plant. But perhaps it is better known as a recreational gathering place for local outdoor enthusiasts. It was here in the late 1800s that curling first began in Amherst, with skating and other winter activities also taking place.

CHILDREN WADING IN CHRISTIE'S POND

By the time the snow melted and summer arrived, locals in the early 1900s would again be drawn to its banks to listen to the bands that played every Wednesday evening from a floating bandstand in the center of the pond. Large crowds of people would rest under the willow trees along the pond's edge, enjoying the music and nibbling on hot roasted peanuts purchased from vendors strolling the bank. The charm of the pond was enhanced when King George and Queen Mary arranged to have a pair of swans delivered to the town to take up residence in the pond. Given the run of the water, the newcomers were duly named George and Mary by local citizens. After freeze-up, they were housed in the basement of West Highlands School. All in all, Christie's Pond was an important place for the early citizens of Amherst.

OUTDOOR CURLING ON CHRISTIE'S POND

OLD

Old Home Week 1910

By 1910, when Amherst celebrated Old Home Week, the population had risen to five thousand, and the town was as prosperous and optimistic of a bright future as it would ever be again. The well-organized gala was a festive time for the town and for the hundreds of former citizens who returned for the celebrations. People were urged to invite friends and relations from away to come home for the great week, and many did. Still, no one could have predicted the overwhelming response to the plans. Train seats and accommodations had to be booked weeks in advance due to the demand, and on opening night, more than one thousand people were turned away from the door of a concert at the Winter Fair buildings. Churches held special services, stores hosted Old Home Week sales, and a "Made in Amherst" exhibit showcasing the town's products caused one leading Boston citizen to remark that it was "better than the Mechanic's Fair in Boston." A 10-mile race, a baseball game, and a variety of other sporting events kept Amherstonians out until all hours, with some said to be

spotted roaming the streets clad only in their nightshirts. A masquerade carnival and fireworks display brought the week to a spectacular and colourful close. A record of the times states that on the closing night of the celebrations, some 15,000 people—three times Amherst's population—witnessed the fireworks display over Christie's Pond. With its floating bandstand, the pond provided the appropriate reflecting pool for the spectacle.

DIAMOND JUBILEE Patriotic occasions over the years tend to have been celebrated on either May 24, July 1, or the first weekend in August. Queen Victoria's long reign from 1837 to 1901 set off a series of Diamond Jubilee celebrations in 1897, but in 1927, it was time for a Dominion Day celebration. It had been sixty years since Confederation. In Amherst, the home of four fathers of Confederation, the mood was particularly joyous and a large crowd gathered to celebrate in Curry Park that July 1. Shown on stage during the official part of the festivities are (L-R) John S. Smiley, Percy C. Black, W.L. Ormond, D.W. Fraser, and Charles R. Smith.

Fred Cameron wins the Boston Marathon

Just five foot three and a mere 116 pounds, Fred S. Cameron was an apprentice machinist who had never before run a race when he finished second at The Regal Athletic Association's annual track meet on Labour Day, 1907 in Amherst. Within a few years, he would be celebrated internationally as a runner, an idea which likely would have seemed preposterous to him at the time. Born November 11, 1886, the son of Joshua and Jane Cameron of Advocate Harbour, Fred grew up fifty miles southwest of Amherst on the Bay of Fundy coast. He was fleet of foot and able to outsprint friends, but there was no athletic program in Advocate schools. The first taste of competition and a credible showing that day in Amherst were enough to get him started though. After catching the attention of Tom T. Trenholm, Amherst's best athletic trainer, he improved and began travelling the Maritime Provinces to race against the region's best.

The Empress on Fire

February 7, 1936 was a dark day in the theatre history of Amherst. On that date, The Empress Theatre—with its large stage, dressing rooms, box seats, and seating for 1,500 people—was destroyed by a fire that was believed to have started in the curtains and staging. The temperature on the night of the blaze was around 20 degrees below zero (Fahrenheit). By morning, after the fire was extinguished, the entire shell of the ruined structure was encased in thick ice. The unfortunate incident was a particularly hard blow to the area since the theatre had played host to everything from high school plays and graduations to travelling companies and variety shows. One of the better-known groups to perform on its stage was the Dumb Bells, a travelling wartime company of men particularly welcome in Amherst since it included a native son, Ross Hamilton.

The Amherst Hotel

Originally located on Amherst's tree-lined Victoria Street, the Amherst Hotel was set back a considerable distance to accommodate coaches and horse-drawn carriages delivering, or belonging to, guests. The hotel was renowned as the first in town to offer room and bath service and, as added incentive, an advertisement in the *Amherst Gazette* of February 2, 1872 announced that the thirty-six rooms operated on temperance principles. By 1911, when it moved to Station Street, business was thriving. Bellhops in tophats and tails greeted guests on solid marble floors and service was said to be impeccable. These days the fate of the circa 1866–67 building with elaborate wrought-iron roof trim and graceful second-storey bay windows is uncertain.

Oscar Wilde at the Lamy Hotel

In 1882, the Irish-born literary giant Oscar Wilde, known for such quotes as "the only way to get rid of a temptation is to yield to it," sought accommodations at Amherst's Lamy Hotel on his second trip to Canada. Prior to the age of motion pictures, radio, and television, entertainment outside the home was largely stage entertainment provided by travelling companies, musicians, lecturers, and local talent. Not surprisingly, Wilde's arrival caused much excitement in the town, and the local newspaper documented his appearance in great detail: "He wore a velvet jacket which seemed to be a good jacket. He had an ordinary necktie and wore a linen collar about number 18 on a neck a half dozen sizes smaller. His legs were in trousers such as Greenfield might have made, and his boots were apparently the product of N.Y. art, judging by their pointed toes. He wore a ring with a seal of a great size. A consensus of the opinions of Amherst people decides that Oscar's hair is not good. It is the colour of straw, slightly leonine, and straight as an Indian's. It is faded and bleached-looking, and when not looked after, goes climbing all over his features. Mr. Wilde was communicative and genial."

TERRACE HOTEL For those seeking a clean and comfortable hotel, with first-class "table" and reasonable rates of $2 daily, Amherst's Terrace Hotel seems to have been the place to go. A 1910 hotel directory advertises the hotel as being the "leading commercial hotel of Amherst," within two minutes' walk of the train depot.

CUMBERLAND HOTEL Nineteenth-century Amherst had a number of hotels to accommodate the needs of visitors, particularly the travelling public. The Cumberland Hotel, located on Princess Street, was one such facility.

MAKING HISTORY

Travelling across Canada is one thing, but making the journey in a car lacking a motor is quite another. Yet, it happened. Friends Frank J. Elliott and George A. Scott made history when they completed the longest tow in the world in a motorless car from one coast to another, a distance of 4,759 miles in 89 days. Their feat is recorded in the *Guinness Book of Records* and in Robert L. Ripley's world-syndicated column, "Believe It or Not."

The story began when the World War One veterans removed the motor from a battered old Model T Ford, rigged a special tow bar and began journeying from Halifax and the Atlantic Ocean on July 18, 1927. Dressed in oilskins and sou'westers, the colourful pair was towed the cross-country distance by 168 friendly motorists, four teams of horses, and two teams of mules. In the days when auto speeds of 30 and 35 miles per hour were considered excessive, motorists took great delight in giving the two men at the end of the tow bar a merry ride on the dirt roads of the time. With limited funds, the enterprising men paid for a portion of the trip through the sale of hundreds of souvenir tin fish, which clattered against the vehicle as it was towed from one destination to another. The fish featured the names of companies who paid a nominal fee to have their business name advertised. After months of travel and international acclaim, the duo ended their once-in-a-lifetime adventure at the Pacific Ocean on October 15, 1927.

Miss Amherst The practice of naming young women to represent small communities was popular in northern Nova Scotia in the 1900s. As this photograph shows, Emma Baker was honoured with the title of Miss Amherst. She later married Percy MacPherson.

Coronation Day Parade Preparations were made throughout the land by towns and villages to mark the occasion of King Edward VII's coronation, and Amherst was no exception. Initially, celebrations were to have been held on June 26th, but the future king's appendicitis forced festivities to be postponed until later in the summer. The new date of August 9, 1902 was marked as a day of general thanksgiving and rejoicing for the new majesties King Edward VII and Queen Alexandra. In Amherst, the parade was a particularly colourful one. Here, the Amherst Fire Department prepares to take part.

Fore! The grand old game's roots in North America were established with the formation of the Royal Montreal Golf Club in 1873, making Canada the birthplace of organized golf on the continent. In 1910, Amherst joined the ranks of golf enthusiasts across the country when the town's first golf club was started by D.S. Biggs and his wife, who together interested their friends in forming an association around the popular sport. Initially, the course was situated on the old Baker farm about a mile and a half below the railway tracks, near the Church of England cemetery. Members travelled back and forth via a covered wagon known as a baroose. Later, the club bought the land shown above, where the course and clubhouse are now located, just outside the town's eastern boundaries.

Greetings From The Elliott Shows and Elliott Family

ELLIOTT SHOWS

With a black bear, an eagle, and a raccoon as attractions, Frank J. Elliott—one of Nova Scotia's best-known showmen—established one of the original carnivals in the Maritimes when he began Frank Elliott Shows in 1921. Known as Shortman, the colourful entrepreneur and his growing family took the popular seasonal show throughout the Maritimes and Quebec every summer. This promotional photo shows the children—Clyde, Glynn, Ron, Wendell, Doreen, Areathea, and Frank Jr.—with their parents, Beatrice and Frank Sr. as well as Lindy the elephant in the background.

Little did they know then that disaster would strike on July 31, 1941 when soldiers at the Debert Encampment destroyed the carnival, leaving only the ferris wheel intact. Lacking insurance to cover the loss, the family spent the next five years playing indoor shows, albeit without the rides for which they were so well known. After five years had passed, the business was re-established when Frank Jr. returned home as a pilot from World War Two. The business underwent another change after a fire in 1964 when brothers Ron and Glynn divided it and formed their own companies: Ron Elliott Shows and Elliott Amusement. The former was sold in 1999 and the latter in 1983, bringing to an end the Elliott's long history in the carnival business.

Amherst Curlers win 20th Century Cup, 1907

Curling in Amherst first began on Christie's Pond in the late 1800s when curlers would take to the outdoor ice for recreation. By the early 1900s, those enthusiasts were prepared to construct a permanent building for their sport. Situated on Eddy Street, the Chignecto Curling Club was used for more than forty years in the early 1900s, with the first Maritime Bonspiel held in 1907 at the former Winter Fair Buildings. Bonspiels were discontinued during the Great War, but continue a proud tradition in Amherst even today. This photo shows the Amherst rink, which won the 20th Century Cup of 1907. Standing L-R: A.M. Bonnyman, first stone and H.W. Rogers, second stone. Seated: W.R. Fitzmaurice, mate, and C.S. Sutherland, skip.

CYCLING Cycling became popular very quickly after it was introduced to the area in the late 1800s. Fred Robb is credited with introducing the first bicycle, a Rover, to Amherst, when he rode it from Sackville, New Brunswick. Meanwhile, the town's first bicycle club was said to have been started by Warren Christie and Percy Sargeant, an amateur photographer and part of the management team at Christie Brothers. A John Wanamaker mail order catalogue of spring 1898 carried an array of models, advertising that "with bicycles, as with horses, there is demand for various kinds. The standard-bred, the thoroughbred, the coach horse, the percheron, the general utility horse—all have clearly defined rights to existence and respect. So this year we meet all bicycle conditions with a string of steeds never equaled before." Bicycles for men, women, and "juveniles" in a variety of models ranged in price from $20 to $125. A tandem sold for $169.

WOMEN ENJOY THIS NEW SPORT

Women, in particular, embraced the advent of cycling. For many in those pre-automotive days, it was their first opportunity for freedom and a chance to get out on their own. A local firm, Robb's Engineering, also made and sold bicycles, making the new sport an accessible one for Amherst area cyclists.

CYCLING BY LAMY HOUSE

Here, cyclists stop for a chat in front of the old Lamy house on Victoria Street East. The structure remains a one-family home.

RAMBLERS MARITIME CHAMPIONS 1905

It's as Canadian as the Maple Leaf, beginning as an adaptation of the Irish field game of hurley and changing to ice hurley and, finally, ice hockey. The Ramblers date back to the late 1800s when a group of boys founded a football club with less than five dollars, which they raised through the collection of bottles and scrap iron. Known initially as the Deceivers, they switched from football to hockey, adopted official red, white, and blue colours, and collected dues of five cents a week to remain solvent. They became the Ramblers around the turn of the century, their colours changing to purple and white. Within ten years, they had their own athletic grounds and a hockey rink—a claim no other sports organization in Nova Scotia could make at the time.

BACK ROW, L-R: L. Simpson, left wing; F. Curran, centre point; A. Lamy, president; F. Brown, point; and E. Curran, right wing.

FRONT ROW, L-R: V. Curry, spare; J. Twaddle, captain and rover; A. Murray, centre; and N. Currie, goal.

Nova Scotia Champs 1906

The Ramblers' baseball team was victorious as champions of Nova Scotia in 1906.

Back row, l-r: V.G. Curry, president; B.S. Corey, pitcher; J.J. Twaddle, centre field; L.H. Curry, centre field; C.D. Currie, right field; A.H. Lamy, secretary.

Middle row, l-r: H. McDonald, shortstop; W.H. Currie, captain and pitcher; N.C. Ralston, third base; and L.A. Simpson, catcher.

Front row, l-r: W.A. Chisholm, first base; C.P. Charlton, second base; and F.T. MacDonald, left field.

The Jeltz Blue Granites

With close ties to the Highland African Methodist Episcopal Church through the energetic Rev. Jeltz, the Jeltz Ball Team was part of the area church league and also travelled within the province to play in exhibition matches against other African/Black ball teams. This baseball team played in Amherst in the 1920s.

Front row, l-r: T. Martin, Oz Lee, Ronnie White (batboy), and Rev. Jeltz.

Second row, l-r: Tracy Izzard, Alton White, Lloyd Ross, and Roy Halfkenny.

Back row, l-r: Gonda Thomas, Herb Halfkenny, Eddie Paris, and Percy Harper.

Amherst Girls' Hockey Team

While the sport of hockey was predominantly a male sport, women in Amherst in the roaring twenties played an active role in their own league. Here are members of the 1924 Amherst Girls' Hockey Team. Top row, left to right: forwards Margaret Brown, Eileen Gallant, and Molly Stevens. Centre row, left to right: right defence Marg Stevens, goaltender Vince McKim, manager E.F. McKim, and left defence Glory McGillvary. Bottom row, left to right: right wing Captain Mutt Webster, centre Millie McCullough and left wing Allie Trenholm.

THE FAIRY QUEEN

The Roach children amused themselves with this innovative goat cart which they called the Fairy Queen. The photo is taken in front of a barn on the 32-acre family farm at 159 East Pleasant Street. The driver is Clara May Roach, who was born in Amherst on October 18, 1899 and lived all her life in the town. The passenger is identified as Earl Thomas Roach, who was born on April 8, 1901 on the family farm where he lived until age 65.

IN THE DRIVER'S SEAT

Clara May Roach was found in the driver's seat once again during this street parade in the early 1900s.

Casey's Boarding House

Boarding houses were common throughout the Amherst area in the early 1900s. Travellers and out-of-town workers attracted to Amherst's industry boom relied on the houses for accommodations while the owners—who tended to be single mothers—often depended on the income provided to make ends meet. In this photo, a young boy and men are seen making music together.

Sunday School Picnic

Sunday School picnics were a popular activity in the early 1900s. In this photo, taken between 1900 and 1905, a group poses for the camera.

EARLY STUDIO PHOTOGRAPHS

These early studio portrayals show the impeccably-dressed Will Charmley and his wife. The photograph of eight-year-old Helen Gay (at right) was taken in 1916. The couple and the young girl were part of the Amherst community of African/Black Nova Scotians, many of whom were among the more than 3,500 free Black United Empire Loyalists whose allegiance to Britain during the American Revolutionary War earned them passage to the province between 1782 and 1784. Another 1,200 or more arrived as the slaves of white Loyalist settlers.

Helen Gay

Waiting at home

The three Martin children—Thorley, Florence, and Margaret—and their mother, Lucy, were patiently waiting at home in Amherst for the return of their father, Lawrence Thorley, who was serving in the No. 2 (Black) Labour Batallion during World War One. Happily, he returned home sometime after this photograph was taken in 1917.

Photo Credits

Photos on pages x, xi, and xv are courtesy of Nova Scotia Archives and Records Management.

Photos on pages 26 and 48 are courtesy of Deane Allen.

The photo on page 32 is courtesy of Janet Christie.

The photo on page 44 is courtesy of Beth Munroe.

The photo on page 50 is courtesy of Ron Elliott.

The photo on page 58 is courtesy of Alex Colville.

Photos on pages 88-90 are courtesy of John McKay.

Photos on pages 114 and 119 (the three Martin children) are courtesy of Lucie Martin-Bishop.

Photos on page 116 are courtesy of Joan Embree Roach.

Photos on pages 118 are courtesy of Donna Morse.

All other photos are courtesy of the Cumberland County Museum.